Being the Organic Self

by

C.C. Elian

Published by C.J. Wishart Media - 2ND EDITION
Cover image of nebula in the constellation of Dorado-150,000 light years: NASA, ESA, and the Hubble Heritage Team (STScI/AURA). Acknowledgement: J. Hughes (Rutgers University)

TABLE OF CONTENTS

INTRODUCTION

> *But I keep thinking that the only thing that can help us now is something that wakes people up deep, down inside, in the place where our ability to understand the world is formed.*
>
> *From Clarity, by Arlene Goldbard.*

WHEN I WAS 16, HEADED EAST AND CROSSING 3RD Avenue on 72nd Street in Manhattan, a question popped to mind that took me over 10 years to answer.

"Sure, there are important questions in life," I thought, "but what is so much a part of the background that no one would ever think to question it?" About a decade later, the answer came, "I would never think to question the words that I was using to compose the thought itself."

That insight was the first step towards an exploration into not only what words are, but how they act as a portal to direct contact with the realities to which they point, not through their meaning, but through the forces that they represent.

Thanks to my longstanding activities and studies in the arts, I was especially well-placed to look at words from many unconventional angles. Over the years, I followed my fascination through different media, from painting, to B&W photography, to music, to video, and eventually to conceptual art in the form of expressive text.

This last phase was the point at which my daily functions and those of my life as a free-form artist blended into one. After several years of using words and concepts as central elements of my artworks, I observed that my way of thinking about reality and of my options within it had changed dramatically. I was increasingly using the same process of looking into the essence of words for both the artworks and for how to manage my daily thoughts and actions.

The insights and understanding that followed from this process not only made life richer, but I could better see the limiting ideas about reality that were enfolded within my problems. I could now go through the words that I used to describe them and into the structural and conceptual forces that bonded them into a reality. This process clarified what solutions were needed so that life's inherent self-healing process could take over with a minimum of resistance from my own self-concepts.

Even more, I saw a direct connection between my inner dialogue's words and how my accompanying feelings were reflected in what happened on the outside. The consistency of this conscious entanglement between inner and outer led to me the viewpoint that, not only is our own life our primary artwork but we can actively participate in its creation. This connection felt completely natural and brought with it a sense of always accessible support from life itself.

The whole process is that of bringing the universal within the grasp of the individual by raising the individual to the level of the universal, and not vice versa.

The Edinburgh Lectures by Thomas Troward

Can others see and live life in this way? Each has to answer that for themselves, and to have that chance they must be able to access the information upon which this viewpoint is based.

By describing the forces involved in many of the keywords that we regularly use, and by introducing the paradigm of a *crossfield of being* as a creative source into which we can tap for co-creation, *Being the Organic Self* offers another way to look at life and at our virtually limitless creative and healing options within it.

When you've tried this paradigm on for yourself, perhaps you will see as I do that the universe is being each of us, one by one. We do not have to journey in isolation so much as live life in collaboration with itself.

To intimately know the words and images by which we live our lives, and dream our dreams is the smoothest way towards their fulfillment. As an inevitable byproduct of this knowledge, we become a fully organic human being that is both sophisticated and untamed. This dual state allows us to navigate not only the external world in which we live, but also our native inner one and in the process, to thrive in both.

C.C. Elian

NB:
The first six chapters describe the conceptual framework and thereafter, each chapter can be read as a stand-alone subject.

1

Immaculate Concepts

Reality is a concept, a specific way of organizing information in order to build up a convincing impression of the world in which we live, each in our own way. Life's day-to-day appearance of being "really" real comes from its 4-Dimensional structures, which engage all the senses that we have. Anything less, such as feelings (1-Dimensional), words or images (2-Dimensional), and imagination (3-Dimensional), never fully satisfy us unless they lead to their 4-Dimensional actuality.[1]

All the same, everything starts without any dimensions at all, as a concept, a reality that we've conceived. What ends up as an object, a feeling, an idea, a meeting, or anything else, always begins as pure undifferentiated energy that is freely available to organize under the forceful effects of informational blueprints. Energy then becomes something that we can call with a word such as: "electron," "ocean," or "hope."

Conceptual blueprints also have the potential to direct energy into collective gestalts, both large and small and so there are paradigm shifts, coincidences, breakthroughs, and revolutions. The roots of them all, things or events, are made from pure potential catalyzed into being through need, desire, creativity, and especially, through imagination.

Whatever comes into being is decided the same way as *King of the Hill*: the being with the most charged presence becomes "really" real—at that particular moment. The search for agreement about any reality is also like an election. The majority vibrations on a theme decide which reality will rule, and the minority vibrations have to go along with it—or else get a majority of their own.

Since most of what we think exists never actually happens in our immediate location, much of what we call "reality" is beyond our capacity to verify. Instead, we must rely on our memories and on information from others to reconstruct what is absent. All the while, we do not doubt that what is out of sight continues after we have moved on.

As a result, most of our reality is carried around abstractly in the form of internalized words, sounds, images. This flowchart of assumptions is the loophole by which reality is only real as a "perceive it forward" creation, something that ceases to exist when we do not interact with it, but is re-created when we do.

Others, meanwhile, are also creating their reality from wherever they are. When we meet them, we each construct bridges of conversation, documentation, images, objects, and so on, in order to create a mutual external world, whereas privately, our respective inner worlds differ vastly.

What seems "normal" to any of us depends upon our 4-Dimensional experiences, in combination with the worldviews that we trust. One of the most powerful views that we can incorporate involves the quantum world. "Powerful" because everything that we physically are, and all that we have arises from this realm of reality where energy hasn't yet decided what it will be when it grows up. Once it does, it becomes the elements of our life story.

Energy at the quantum level is seemingly in an undetermined state until someone starts to interact with it. At that point, its multiple-choice potential is reduced to one certainty. The core concepts held by the observer create an energized and informed state that emerges as the specifics of a given reality. The forces that exist at the quantum level lead to phenomena such as observer-dependent results, entangled particles, and counterintuitive superpositions of multiple states (yes + no + maybe) These quantum terms will be covered in simplified fashion in a subsequent chapter.[2]

> *One consequence of the theory of quantum mechanics is that events in the past that were not directly observed did not happen in a definite way. Instead they happened in all possible ways... Unless forced to choose a particular state by direct interference from an outside observation, things will hover in a state of uncertainty. Review of a book by Stephen Hawkins.* [3]

Even a simple grasp of the quantum world and its mechanics can give you a clear sense of energy's freedom before it is made to shape our everyday reality. From this understanding you too can conclude that all outward events are directly dependent upon those that occur inwardly, within us. To "get" this relationship is our key to effective conceptual techniques that permit us to transform our day-to-day experiences into their optimal processes and outcomes.

A direct cause & effect relationship like this is possible because any reality is first an undulating turf of vibrations, one whose fluctuating forces are what determine the life landscapes that we must travel. This same principle exists in music, whereby an implied story line emerges from a given sequence of notes. Change the notes and the melodic story must also change. In our case, the "notes" consist of our thoughts, feelings, actions, and our all-important imagination.

QUANTUM = QUIDQUID[4]

Until the natures of quantum properties became undeniable, there was no division between "standard model" physics and those at the quantum level. That's why physics could be described as "laws," that is: seemingly inescapable forces, unlike social laws, which are more or less force-backed rules, alterable at will by political and private entities.

In a parallel way though, just as social rules dictate human motions, the laws of physics are strong rules that govern how beings can move in relation to one another. Moreover, as with social laws, their dynamics can be recombined once their mechanisms are understood. That's because anything termed a "law," be it social or organic, is based on forces that shape what *can* be rather than what *must* be.

A full and free life is all about conceptual techniques; how to think about ourselves and life is the path to discovering and benefiting from our reality's flexible and transmutable properties. In order to shape our reality we must strip our experiences down to their conceptual foundations. From that perspective, we can reconfigure events without predominantly going through real time requirements but instead, by working through our processes of feeling, thinking, and imagining.

Problems usually come when we take the rules of life's games too literally and hypnotize ourselves into thinking that there is no way out of an undesirable reality. There is always a way out... but first we need to think so.

The conceptual basis of life as a technique for directing our own experiences is not yet a mainstream one, and consequently, those putting it into practice are pushing towards new boundaries. This trailblazing is no different an innovation than when electricity finally came from solar cells instead of through transformers. As with solar energy, this conceptual technology gives us a lighter footprint, autonomy, and uncomplicated comfort.

Keep in mind that although we get to experience the exhilaration of the creative process, we must sometimes also navigate the poignancy of letting go. Life relies upon such a contrast to offer all creations its full spectrum of special effects.

2

Rules of a Game

"Hackers are the 1%, the elite and the creators," said Clarke. White House cybersecurity adviser [5]

To direct the system from within, we don't need to push against a given reality's concrete way of being, we just need to use the leverage that its conceptual underpinnings offer us.

3

Let it be Light

To connect to life's potential for creativity, we first need to open our minds to the idea that transforming ourselves and the reality that we experience is the biggest part of our humanity and of its immune system—that it is a part of our need for self-actualization and health. To direct this creativity, conceptual and verbal techniques are necessary. Just as with the successful application of any technique, the results will be sensual and not mechanical.

Our personal and creative powers in life first depend upon the way in which we think about ourselves and the nature of reality. These two paradigms affect how we react to our life's situations and their key words. This book offers a structure-based frame about some of them so that we can liberate ourselves from automatic meaning and instead, practice a form of conceptual aikido by dealing with words' forces. Meanings are individual and only arise after we have a belief about how reality supposedly works, whereas forces are the same everywhere.

Most keywords are familiar: *identity, ego, love, truth, consciousness, money, meaning, trust, now, spirituality, faith, matter, reality*. Many of these are usually discussed as philosophical subjects—something about which we can have an opinion but without any universal agreement as to their objective descriptions. All words, however, are conceptual building blocks whose shaping potential is directed by how clearly we grasp the emotional and intellectual structures that a given word is about.

Not just keywords, but all words are informational blueprints that play their role in physicality's construction of specific forms and relationships, each one a variation on the theme of Being. Each word's transformational effects cut both ways such that by rephrasing a thought we can free ourselves from an idea's hold on our self-evaluation—or else sentence ourselves to manufactured limitations by overlooking the language of our insecurities. The more objectively we can look at what a word's forces are about, the easier our understanding of its role in our life and of our options to dispel its effects upon us or conversely, reinforce them for our benefit.

We don't need to strong-arm things into change, because once we understand what is at the root of our situation then the needed transformations happen as a matter of course. The important word here is "understand": to stand under and see the original seeds from where something takes on being. In whatever way that is, we will describe our thoughts and feelings in words. The more we understand these words, the better we can resolve and transform any matter.

> *But his research of the last 15 years has convinced him that hydra can, in fact, survive forever and are "truly immortal." Genetically hydras are the same as human beings. We're variations of the same theme.*[6]

Each person can shape their reality in the same way that an artist shapes their chosen medium, namely: from the desire to do so. As does an artist, to become an expert in our medium we need to understand the materials that we use to create with, in this case: concepts as delivered via words and images.

What we think about our life, and how we feel about it, comes from clothing ourselves in textiles spun from our concepts of self and reality. As our conceptual texts and emotional textures unceasingly formulate one another, the patterns of our life emerge from the fibers of our feelings in cross-weave with those of our self-concepts.

Although we may think of ourselves primarily as a specific person, our core is a self-directed consciousness that willingly undertook a human journey to come under the spell of its own experiences. Identity and personhood are simply a means towards that end.

Each of us started our life with the seed of a goal: the fulfillment of our authentic self, the one that can never sever its connection to its deepest sources of being because it emerges out of a unity of all beings. As with all voyages we cannot guarantee how or if we will ever reach our destination because, once we incarnate, we must then cross the forces of the actual path itself towards the goal.

In the process, we run into unprecedented situations and unavoidably, go further and further out on a limb of material extensions. These experiences develop our custom-tailored strengths of lifestyle and character that determine if we will maintain our seed goal in its rightful place at the center of our heart.[7]

This ongoing challenge is not extraordinary; it is simply part of navigating the circumstances and temptations of life. Although the universe will unfailingly respond to whatever we do, it nonetheless has no agenda as to what we each *should* do with our lives. Rather, it is up to us to nurture the concept of a caring universe so as to create our half of a bridge that life then crosses to deliver to us its support and resources.

To have the capacity to transform any moment's textures, we must return to the realization of our basic self as a purely conceptual being constantly defining and refining itself through our exercises of imagination and our belief in various kinds of information.

With such a lighter-than-air conceptual viewpoint, we can readily imagine the arrival of any moment's ideal transformation as easily as a sculptor envisions the next curve of a figure.

The capacity to make use of our native creativity exists to the extent that we can commute between the freeform inner world and the relatively constant outer one, each of which is an aspect of the other. Together, inner and outer shape a seamless feedback spiral, an energetic stream. [8]

What transforms us into an authentic artist is our continuous remembrance of this ongoing interflow and our courage to seize each moment's self-expressive and healing options. These can take many forms, but all creativity involves our awareness of the changes that we cause with each movement, with each thought, with each feeling. This includes the creativity that we exercise when living any kind of a life, not just that of a professional artist.

Your brain continuously compares the information that comes in through your eyes with what it expects on the basis of what you know about the world. [9]

Once we realize that all the segments of our daily lives emerge from the inside out, then we can learn to see how each moment is drawn out according to what we feel we deserve, and in the way that we feel we deserve it. The concept of "drawing out" reality is particularly fitting because, as with the act of sketching, life is an art form that appears upon fresh pages marked with the neurological firings that depict our inner and outer motions.

To look at our life dynamics in this way requires the ability to detach from being a solid "me" into being a neutral and observing consciousness, one in contact with sensory information but not identified with it. Not because detachment is a righteous stance, but for the sake of pragmatism.

Only from a place that offers perspective can we both deconstruct and reconfigure the conceptual arrangements that define what our lives are about at any given moment. Just as a painter by stepping back determines where a painting needs the next compositional element, so our stance as an observing consciousness lets us compose ourselves at will. This approach is especially essential if we do not want to live at the mercy of the many self-serving forces originating from the beings and concepts around us.

We develop this engaged detachment by cultivating a parallel presence in our inner world, which is where our observations can notice the shifting concepts of self and reality that are holding it all together. Our insights into the lynch-pin ideas and emotions involved in any situation then trigger inspiration for creative techniques that further our desired outcomes of reality.

Such an optimal relationship with our perceptions maintains a neurological flow of unhesitating synaptic firings that keep us moving "through" experiences rather than being stumped by them. The smoother the process, the more we can simultaneously direct and observe the way in which anything arises, from concept to full manifestation.

In parallel, detachment develops the capacity to act deliberately rather than reactively. It does so because whenever we increase inner space, we reduce the speed of outer changes. With seemingly fewer external demands, we can now consider our actions while fully receptive to our intuitions and their guidance.

Although detachment is a major part of our technical repertoire, the goal of life is still to live fully immersed in it, just not so much as to become lost and confused about what is going on and how it happened. Once we can think of our reality in terms of creative potential molded into being by a variety of formative forces, then we begin to find our expressive freedom. To benefit from this, however, we must still incorporate its realizations into our daily lives. We start by being aware of how we think about things.

Thinking is a highly developed form of technology, a means of experiencing reality in virtual form. Through specialized mirror neurons, our nervous system registers any reality to the degree of existence that our imaginations and perceptions believe it has.[10] Consequently, whatever seems "really" real instantly urges us towards or away from action: our heart races when sounds in the dark "are" footsteps that shadow us, only to calm itself once we realize that our pursuer is simply a windblown leaf.

Thinking's mechanisms depend on yet another technology, that of language, which functions to define our perceptions according to how deeply we understand the forces embodied within our own life's keywords. The first step towards a deep consideration of these words is to realize how meaningless they are on their own. Words derive their vitality only from the sensory experiences that they indicate. The more we understand this, the more effectively we can both use our own and understand others' words.

Apart from humans, life doesn't need words to exercise its vitality since it gets its information through each being's physicality. With people however, life's creativity needs not only words, but images as well. These are the two primary forms of information manipulated by our imaginations–itself shaped by our heart's cumulative content.

When we see words as 2-Dimensional arrows that point away from themselves towards their subject, then we know that eventually, we must receive our information directly from the sensory 4-Dimensional situations to which they point. Within these is where we actually live, and not from our ideas about them. These last are missing the final fourth dimension of direct experience.[11] Whenever we become unchaperoned by dogmatic text, we can now make naked contact with the sensory nature of each moment. Fully free to feel and sense, we become wildly vitalized and act with vigor, instinct, and imagination.

For the profound timing and guidance that inevitably develop, this synthesis of our native animal neurology with our socialized literate self is the ideal organic human state. Only pure animals can act in the moment with their whole being, unhindered by concepts of what *should* happen. Instead, each instant is addressed with the totality of their senses' capacities for action and instinct. Then as a counterpoint, our literacy acts to balances the scales away from the potential savagery of raw animal being and offers understanding as to context and its inherent consequences.

When we are in our own (what I call) humanimal state, we also sense the process of living as an evolving dialogue between life's energies and ourselves. Accordingly, our resistance is at a minimum as to what is and as to what might be next.

The easy give & take that flows from our relaxation liberates us from the impression of a forced storyline to each situation. Consequently, we no longer feel the need to play out the seemingly conventional causes and effects of any kind of a situation. Instead, we behave with inspiration and spontaneity. In the process we are increasingly comfortable to be in suspense and to let life unfold into the adventure that it always has the potential to be.

As a result, we no longer need to restrain ourselves in self-protection from the future, nor in reaction to the past. Instead, we can focus our energies on growth and expansion within our own now and not someone else's, which might be quite different. Each present moment is when every component of our life is in real time contact with its own information, when all of its zero to 4 dimensions are lined up, available for our experience and subject to our directions. Only during this moment of Now is there an open channel for pure energy to flow to its called for destination as our personally guided manifestation.[12]

From this powerful stance, we naturally act in a state of sensory wonder whereby we experience both the innocence of a child, and the sophistication of an adult. Our accompanying lack of resistance to existence, which is infancy's hallmark thirst for life, lets perception, sensuality, and spontaneous information flow into our consciousness. This way of life needs neither belief systems nor renunciation, only information and our deliberate use of it.

We are on this earth on a temporary basis; it is our responsibility and ours alone, to care for our life and the fulfillment of its potentials. How much of it we actualize and in what way, depends upon our access to information, our ability to differentiate the various forms that it takes, followed by what information we either ignore or act upon.

4

THE CROSSFIELD OF BEING

What sometimes hinders the precision of the shot is the archer's over-active will. He thinks: 'What I fail to do will not be done', and that's not quite how things work. Man should always act, but he must also let other forces of the universe act in their own due time.[13]

ALTHOUGH THE CONVENIENCES OF socialization encourage us to think in linear terms of discoverable cause and effect, our experiences show us that life is multi-dimensional, non-linear, and readily interactive. If you haven't noticed this yet, just look for evidence of it in your own experiences and you will easily find it.

Rather than credit the fact of life to a creator who has a separate being from its creations, the paradigm of a crossfield of being views all existence as based upon a creative force that is willingly streaming itself into individuality. The universe works as a collaboration of interconnected parts, not one of which is the creator of the rest of them but rather, all of them create the oneness of each thing, including you and me.

Life's oneness diverging into multiple individuals of all kinds, from atoms to rocks, to people, to stars, is an arrangement that allows each creation to be immersed into its own way of being and to interact authentically with other equally immersed creations.

The crossfield of being is simply a more tangible way of describing what others would call "God," "the Universe," or "Source." In essence, it is a neutral force that is creating what we call "reality", and to which we can consciously be connected, one that we can interact with at will for the sake of transforming our experiences. Think of it as another one of those fields that we can tap into, just as we do with the all-pervasive electromagnetic spectrum from which (if we know how) we can extract waves of electricity, radio, infrared, UV, and so on.

From the crossfield of being we can extract guidance, energy, insight, synchronicity, healing, inspiration, etc. Unlike the electromagnetic fields, we don't need external equipment to interact with the crossfield and receive its contents; our own existence is the transformer of this field's potential. To make use of it we simply need to be self-aware of the ongoing conceptual process of our daily lives and accept the responsibility of guiding it either into or away from action.

Within this paradigm, we humans exist because a crossfield of being (aka Source, aka God,) has conceived itself into multitude forms of life. It has done so as part of its own acting-out of infinite creative self-expression—a motivation that characterizes all existence.

In fairness to any experience that might well include difficulties, this source of being is not only available as our collaborator for maintaining the well being in our lives, but especially for surmounting the challenges that we encounter, no matter how great.

The crossfield is a "root directory" of zero-dimensional concepts whose blueprints have the potential to vitalize and guide the individuality of each being. As a major part of their instincts for wellbeing and fulfillment, all forms of life automatically tap into and add their own experiences to this database. Humans are in both a privileged and disadvantaged position. The first because, thanks to their free will, they can bring into being almost whatever their imaginations conceive of. However, thanks to that same free will, they can restrict their own innate connection and fail at their creations, or even ignore that they have any options at all.

The crossfield also gathers all forms of information as they are generated from each being's existence and its particulars. Whatever information any creation processes and generates adds itself to this pool of data. The crossfield's receptivity to information on any matter, at all levels, and under all circumstances, is infinite; it just needs a spring in order to expand. One of life's circular ironies is that our source also needs its sources.

No form of being or subject matter is excluded: if something takes up space, regardless of size or place, imaginary or concrete, it participates in generating information. In this way, each individual existence both contributes to, and benefits from, the collective.

Unlike destructive variations in life, the crossfield thrives regardless of what is added to it and therefore, contains in equal measure information that we desire, as well as that which we hope never to know. This is to say that not all information is only pleasant, and how all information is being put to use depends upon the spirit in which it is being used.[14]

Since information's potential to manifest into 4-Dimensionality is only latent, all this information is tapped into at a point, that which we call "now"- itself an intersection of vertical and horizontal fields: a *crossfield*, rather than either an exclusively horizontal or vertical one. To go beyond the zero dimensionality of pure conceptual form, information has to be vertically drawn out by a "calling" force of some kind such as: need, desire, distress, or imagination. This calling can come from any sort of being, anywhere, and at any time.

As each point in space is instantaneously and endlessly updated with new information, this crossfield is omnipresent and accessible in its totality throughout the universe. The all-inclusive crossfield of being is why divination methods and religious belief systems work for their believers. Any such systems are a way of giving ourselves permission to access information that is already available to us.

However, the entry fee for any human religion is that we must accept its templates for our identity, along with its arbitrary conditions for our self-worth and right to tap into needed resources. A freer alternative to such limiting systems is for us to claim our individual identity as an extension of life itself, and to incorporate the crossfield's omniscient and omnipotent resources into our daily life.

Thanks to this reunion with our source, we are now able to draw out the energy, guidance, and specific information needed to fulfill the text of our deepest life story—the one latently written within the unique purpose of our earthly arrival. We can also catalyze external events in the form of coincidences, synchronicities, and fortuitous meetings.

Information is deeper than reality.
Anton Zeilinger, Physicist.

At this point, we no longer need to edit our life stories along generic scripts, but only according to our own inspired authenticity—which in our optimism to incarnate we thought we'd be able to do, regardless of the challenges that we knew awaited us. This synthesis of our organic and deeply informed being provides us with the conceptual tools needed to create our ideal life without doing so at the expense of others. On the contrary, our self-actualization increases the health and richness of the world, one being at a time.

This creative empowerment is possible because life's convincing presence is a feat of conceptual technology, one that only simulates the 4-Dimensional physicality we experience as reality. What seems real is like characters on a screen, and in our case; one constructed by our senses under the influence of whatever information reaffirms our concepts of self and of reality.

Ultimately, life is a directed dream and each of us a creative dreamer. Lived as an art form, reality requires us to awaken within the dream, to create with opened eyes, and do so in the service of our heartfelt goals, which at deeper levels will include elements that benefit the totality.

5

Day Dreaming

We live with the impression that reality's material is solid. That the objects and their processes are dense, concrete and if we don't physically alter them, that they will remain as they are. This is an illusion, one intended to create just the right amount of tension such that things "matter". In fact, things are all subject to change, to transformation, and to disappearance through our ways of thinking about them.

Just as in a lucid dream, our reality can be reconfigured when we awaken to the creative control that we have over our day to day experiences. [15] The difference between everyday living and a lucid dream is simply one of proportions. In sleep dreams, our self-aware "I" is much less in control than is the surrealistic momentum of our dreaming state. In contrast, during awakened reality, our "I" is the great leader and reality's surrealistic freeform options far smaller–the size of a loophole.

All the while, just as we lucidly dream only when we are actually asleep, so only when we are truly awake in the moment can we direct our own stories. This requires us to be mindful within that most-evasive moment called "now."

As described later in depth, every reach into a Now occurs while that moment's elements are in their most charged and self-realized state; that is: when now's information in the form of its contents is fully aligned and flowing into the next moment. It's similar to a situation when you see someone you know and want to speak with them; that's the moment when the potential to have that conversation is at its most vivid. Similarly, now is when we can interact with its contents to effect a desired change. Now is when we can extend our imagination's reach into the crossfield and draw out guidance for the needed steps towards the transformations that we want.

The moment of Now is that point when all the activated dimensions of "what is" are present and shaping themselves towards what eventually become our life stories. It's our choice whether or not to assume the responsibility of acting upon the current contents of our now and taking them towards the future that we really want—or if we like what is in our now, of making sure that it is ongoing.

Keep in mind that the process of creation is neutral as to what is being drawn out, it only responds to degrees of intensity. The most charged imagination calls the loudest, and its vibrations will be those that first aggregate into materiality. When directing our moment to moment experiences we need to be aware if we are reaching for what we want, or else bracing ourselves for what we fear.

For those of us who live with the effects of trauma or anxiety, we too easily expect danger and stress, so we will need to encourage ourselves in baby steps to trust that we can heal and create a fulfilled life. It's no different a process than lifting weights. At first we might be so weak as to be able to lift only a small amount, but if we are consistent, then our strength is guaranteed to develop, and in less time than you think.

Instead of physical weights, we will be lifting images and ideas of wellbeing that might in the moment feel very far out of reach. This is temporary, and as we practice holding in mind desired ideas, it will become ever easier to keep them in sight.

For encouragement and reassurance, if you can regularly get away to a park or areas of nature to watch and to listen, or at a minimum by watching movies of nature, you will see how generously life offers vitality to every creature and plant, how inherent to life are beauty and ingenuity. With such examples, we can readily reach for our preferences rather than for what we dread because we will see that life's primary thrust is always towards wellbeing & satisfaction—towards health, whose root meaning is "wholeness."

Vitality is all that we *can* create, for death is the absence of life and not something that we can bring into being, rather it's the consequence of a withdrawal of life. This dynamic is simply a form of economy. That all beings should get what they need and desire is a far more efficient system than that of forcing them into insufficiency and desperation. Such conditions only pressure a being's overall system into disrepair rather than towards regeneration. It takes a lot more energy to restore decay to well being than it does to maintain a healthy state.

What usually blocks people's fulfillment is not the lack of means for achieving it but rather their own sense of not deserving happiness, even though feeling good is the constant goal of every being. Except for humans, all life forms reach without hesitation for what they most want. Nature's example of how its creatures always seek their satisfaction offers us the assurance that if we nurture our highest potential, then our own being will be oriented towards more vitality, more resources, and more self-actualization.

As it is with all other beings, we will not undergo this process alone; nor can we, no matter how dark the night. Any sense of personal solitude is only a by-product of our social and ultimately, fictional identity. Our stand-alone status is part of life's special effects, which are in place to create the illusion of an individual life story. Every such narrative needs a lead character, and in your life, you're it.

Just as a movie intends to tell a story that seems real, life's reality also needs stable, external points of reference. Without a logical, hard chain of seeming causation, there could be no sense of tension and consequently, we could resonate neither emotionally, nor physically, nor intellectually. Instead, everything would feel fleeting and ungraspable, irrational, as in sleeping dreams. To experience concrete things, we want and need edges in life, just not so sharp that we bleed away our life force and cut ourselves off from our creative options.

We ignore reality's flexible nature when we mistakenly consider its boundaries to be hard and absolute. These seem to become even harder—and often, harsher—when we have let a situation's inertia continue unchecked—ironically, at which point we need reality's flexibility the most. Yet, just as readily as it is made dense, reality's hard core can be dissolved to reveal imagination and longing as our life's chief engineers and builders.

The specifics of every reality directly reflect the orchestration of the experiencer's root vibrations, both conceptual and emotional. When we change the way in which we tune ourselves, we alter the next moment's formative pulsations. Subsequent revisions in our story will then emerge as solidly as do those that follow a writer's selection of different words to tell a different tale.

What becomes a real thing is only the final expression of what emerged from a conceptual field whose vibratory landscapes form the first dimension of our feelings. As we contact ever-greater dimensionality, we draw out 2-Dimensional words and images, which are then illustrated in the 3-Dimensionality of our imaginations and, finally, the 4-Dimensions of our life's events.

As soon as we open ourselves to the idea of reality as principally constructed from pure concepts, then we can put this way of thinking into effect. It is usually beyond this point when we seem to receive offers of assistance through fortuitous circumstances, or new information. Life offers supportive resources to all who connect with its source, regardless by what name we call it: God, the Universe, the Crossfield. The only requirement is to seek out this connection. Again, you don't have to believe in the crossfield for this dynamic to work; it is simply another convenience for talking about the fact of being alive and the interactive options life offers us to shape it.

"I think Carmen... and my mother.... are kindred spirits," said Righter. "I think the universe conspired somehow to bring together these two women." [16]

Simultaneously with our reach for it, the crossfield is meeting us halfway and extending its own information into verticality of being. It thus informs energy into becoming the changes that we want to flow to us. These come through meetings, coincidences, sudden opportunities, and new ideas. The crossfield also brings us the insight and understanding needed to make the most of these encounters.

Many of us have experienced urgent prompts to do something or go somewhere at a certain time, but without any obvious reason; as a result, we resisted letting ourselves be moved into action. Yet, those who did so found that a benefit awaited them, sometimes a great one. With a history of intuition-driven accomplishments, we eventually realize that we ignore these directives to our own disadvantage.

The support offered by the crossfield of being does not do away with the process of going through any of our experiences. If it did, then there would be no point at all in the limitations within which we live. It would be like being in a random slide show with no reason for one image to lead to another. Alternatively, via the crossfield in its collaboration with our own initiative, we get to play the game of life with an optimal set of cards, regardless of circumstances.

We can get a sense of this living support by observing the skill of other creatures in constructing their habitats, finding food, communicating with one another, and acting on a multitude of other useful intuitions. These activities are in response to an immediate now as it relates to each entity's streaming sensory information.[17]

We can tap into that same assistance for whatever we need to feel fulfilled–no matter how trivial or silly. This bounty is possible specifically because of reality's base as vibratory events–our life is simply a stabilized dream. As a result, in terms of energy expenditure, it doesn't matter what comes into being since none of it is ultimately there.

When everything is seen as an arrangement of blueprinted energies, then the cost for materializing what we wish applies to our own self-management rather than to a competition with others for limited resources.

6

Being Human

To be human is to be quantum.[18]

The idea that most of our lives are controlled by outer physicality is inaccurate. "Inner" and "outer" are necessary concepts for anything's hardline definition but they are not mutually exclusive realms. Reality is a play of forces without any inner or outer separation between its parts. The same entity plays them all: pure energy of "Being" acting under the influence of information.

For the game to play itself in full however, it is necessary that all the players partially forget their unity; only in this way can life offer self-rule for each creation to act and "be" completely as it is. The status of individuality is a device that lets information be uploaded to the crossfield from a multitude of unique sources of data, be they atoms or astronauts.

We human beings are at the cutting edge of life's own infinite self-expansion, and extremely essential to its process. A variety of physical presences capable of deconstructing, then of reconstructing their environment's elements is vital to life's own evolution, to its reach for more information, ever faster, ever more nuanced.

Thanks to our capacity for abstract thought, an upright stance, opposable thumbs, and others attributes, we humans are free to recombine whatever we can into unprecedented situations and objects. We do so through the imagination that fills our individual inner worlds. Within that unique space, cause and effect, as well as external laws of materiality can be bypassed. Here, all things play out their variations on the theme of creatively shaped energy.

Our own main goal is not primarily to increase information for the crossfield but rather to customize our life story and so, experience the sensory manifestations of our needs and longings. The resultant uploads of information are simply an automatic by-product of this free-will creativity.

Due to the crossfield's infinite pool of information, we are forced to edit our lives, much as a novelist focuses on one storyline rather than another. In the same way, we center on the characters and situations illuminated by our perceptions. We eventually turn these high points into the key elements of our story—from which other generations extract their own highlights and turn it into history.

Regardless of how it is written, any story is mostly fictional since, according to what role they are given each situation's details had the potential to change the direction and tone of what was being written. Only our own style and personality in the moment decides what is selected. And selections must be made because if you cannot identify and describe something, then you cannot relate to it—what then remains are pure sensations, which is how non-human creatures experience life.

To speak of consciousness without describing its subject matter is the same as talking about light without mentioning the thing upon which it shines. Without a subject to illuminate, light and consciousness both remain invisible. Consequently, the more precise we are in how we perceive and describe the elements of our moments, the more conscious we are.[19] Because of their capacity for literacy, human beings are at the upper end of having the necessary biology and culture to deliberately tap into the crossfield. Every other being can also access it–in fact, they cannot avoid doing so. They too arise out of it, are guided by it, and add to it. The difference is: non-human creations cannot extract raw materials and then, recombine them as quickly as an engineer or an artist might do–including, just for the fun of it.

That said, what other creations can do especially well is process sensory information in a completely unresisting way, which is in sharp contrast to human beings. In most of us, this skill of sensing "what is" at tonal levels becomes instead ideas that we project into the future or else, pull out from the past. For other creatures, their contact is purely in a streaming now.

EVENTUALLY

Before I was born here, I had a sister, right? Her and my other Mom are so old now. They were OK when the car was on fire, but I sure wasn't! [20]

We do not reincarnate so much as we get recycled. In whatever way we once lived, the crossfield offers other beings access to the sensory information that we generated. During our lifetime, whenever we move through spaces and situations, whatever we experience and express, all of it leaves an imprint of information that becomes available to someone else, somewhere else, even at another century.

What we do and think, even when it occurs in the privacy of our inner world, becomes new material that other beings use for the sake of their own authenticity. The unfulfilled dreams, the paths not taken, the regrets, the blind and the illuminated spots of consciousness that characterized our lives, all become potential material for another person's story. At the end of their span, each being's life-forces settle to their ground level, similarly to fallen leaves decomposing in the forest. Their raw materials then benefit those life forms that continue. Like oil made from compressed vegetation, each person's essence becomes the fuel for another's drive.

What has already been lived also endures as source material for both historical and fictional characters. Authors not only research but also dip their pens into the residual pool of what, and who, once existed. However unnoticed your life may seem to be, it will not remain so forever. In the works of say: a novelist, a filmmaker, a painter, a poet, or a composer, there may well be a character or story formed through the life that you have experienced, perhaps even the life of another person who is what you wished you could be.

This gate to other's material is not just for the use of practicing artists, but also for individuals yet to be. Our yearning for the paths not taken become someone else's imperative, either in the future, or in the past. You therefore have the child prodigy who only wants to play their music, the devoted parent who foregoes a career track, or a libertine who cares nothing for self-restraint. The possibilities are endless. What drives the individual in these instances is the quest for a certain tonality of sensory information, one with which they already resonated at birth.

These re-incorporated elements, which were once a part of someone's unity, can be reframed as reincarnation or as karma. They can also be framed as raw creative potential ready to find a host, the same as apple seeds are left to their fates on the ground, to succeed or not, according to the specifics of weather, animals, and soil.

7

Hand Over Your Heart

Come on, have a heart...

Our heart is the whisperer who tells us the story of our longings; it is the receiving station for all our neurological impressions—a terminal that synthesizes our various life experiences into the stories that describe us to ourselves and to others. Within our heart is where we summarize which life stories embody our ideals and which do not. The heart is where we either encourage or discourage ourselves.

"Encourage" is a fitting word because its root meaning is directly about giving strength to the heart, whose own goal is to seek the fulfillment of the being that encases it.[21] This is only natural; the heart has a strong stake in its host's joys and sorrows since these sensations will inevitably be processed through it.

The heart's leadership is in direct response to our nervous system's activations, which are always prompting us towards a self-affirming life, towards being happy even when we can only feel miserable. Our very misery comes from how far away we are from what we long for.

Regardless of the heartfelt territory that we need to cross, its destination remains the same: all our experiences are based on inner blueprints that seek to construct a life of joy and well-being. When we ignore our heart's movements or deliberately suppress them, then our happiness' defeat is enabled from within.

When someone says: "follow your heart," they're lobbying (sometimes, vicariously) for us to act on scenarios that we have mapped out in our imaginations—a neurological territory of dreams and goals. Such advice recognizes that to ignore information coming from the heart is to ignore oneself on vital subjects, and at one's peril.

To follow our heart is to let the natural flow of our neurology play itself out, which happens sometimes smoothly and other times in a rough and tumble way. The actualized contents of our heart can temporarily initiate disorder when their release appears after a lengthy suppression. This process cannot be helped; the heart must empty itself of its disappointments before it can fill itself with real joy. Though it will eventually do so, we cannot initially assume that following our heart will first lead to happiness.

Our heart's assumptions that specific conditions or people bring happiness can be based on impressions that may not be accurate—I offer petitions for divorce as one proof. Such miss-impressions are normal: we cannot know how a fulfilled wish actually feels until it appears and we get to experience its aftertaste. Only life makes of us better estimators.

In the end, we are always best off acknowledging what is in our heart, for even if getting what our heart desires does not provide exactly what we expected, the liberation of our pent-up feelings and consequent emotional release results in a great benefit to our entire system. Consequently, we become existentially lighter and move within a quieter and more efficient inner atmosphere. Though it is sometimes challenging, this clearing of the air is a precondition to the heart's fulfillment, and an essential part of any heart's healing.

Whenever we persist in leading with our heart then we will

eventually come to a place where it can finally live what it has yearned for. This homecoming may not have the landscape or face that we thought it would, but once it finally appears, we recognize it for what it is.

Time is no object for our heart's quest. Whatever potential we've ignored for a heartfelt life is always prepared to manifest itself when the opportunity comes, or is forced into being. Sometimes our unexpressed needs and desires are so strong that in one way or another they explode. We then find ourselves within an extraordinary transformation, initiated by a seemingly small action. "It just happened..." is the phrase often heard. Not really.

What took place is that the emotional pressure in our heart seized upon an opening and rushed out to gratify long-standing yearnings. This often appears as the mid-life crisis and comes from a sense that it is "now or never" for major dreams to find their realization.

Difficult and complicated as some of these situations are, our existence will remain incomplete unless we experience life in full actualization, that is to say: with all our heart. Until then, we cannot feel what it is to be full of life. Ultimately, we must follow our heart if we want to integrate all that we go through and from that, recognize what is beneficial to us and what is best discarded.

In the process of following where our heart takes us, we often find that earlier life impressions feel outdated. Amid once-familiar words and places, our heart's emotional trail leads us to the silhouette of a self that is no longer how we are. Apparently, our nervous system, and therefore our heart, changed from what it once so clearly was. We now resonate to different self-concepts than before. These experiences have a high value because, whenever we update our heart's impressions, we simultaneously enhance our capacity to live ever more spontaneously in the present.

HEART + MIND + HEART + MIND +

The advice to follow one's heart is incomplete unless it specifies the inclusion of our thoughts in the process. For a lasting fruition, our heart's emotional information must join forces with our mind's reactions to it. Otherwise, we either have the blind rushing-in of children (who naturally take things to heart), or the cold decision of someone disconnected from their feelings, and so, who acts heartlessly.

To minimize our disenchantments, this heart-mind union is, in fact, mandatory. The sensing nature of the heart cannot rationally examine in detail what is going on with itself; it can only speak in terms of feelings and emotions. In contrast, the detached nature of the thinking mind cannot fully appreciate the emotional consequences of its own purely analytic assessments.

The ideal partnership then, is for the heart & mind to cooperate such that the form desired by the heart is one that its partner-mind knows can deliver the goal-content. In the process, the heart and mind protect one another from their respective blind spots.

Regardless of their contrasting styles, the actions of both have the same outcome in mind, or at heart: that of creating a full and rich life for the person who contains them and who must deal with each one's influences. Stripped down to their basic characters, the heart can be described as our wild animal being and the mind as our domesticated one.

Like a wild creature, the heart cannot be forced against its truth into a feeling or desire. If neither is there, no force on earth can instill them. Only the mind can rationalize itself into action, but not the heart. On the other side, what the heart loves generates unrestrained forces, never mind the cost. The heart is associated with love precisely because of love's neurological basis as a receiving station for any information on the beloved.[22]

Once a person's heart is in love, their energy is at its most inspired and efficient. They exercise no efforts in being involved, nor do they doubt when it is time to act. They are free to truly be alive and by their example, to encourage life in others.

8

ME ME ME ME ME

ANYONE CAPABLE OF READING these words is as much a synthetic creation as the words themselves. There is no such spontaneous creature as a socialized person, any more than there is a natural book. Social moulding transforms us from raw animals into somewhat civilized people. An identity has to be constructed and it subsequently shapes our roles within the staged theater that is every society.

Without some form of socialization, a human being would live along the same lines as any creature; namely, to provide almost exclusively for their physical nourishment and safety. For example, children left to grow in the wild have little potential for becoming socialized. Their limited neurological and cognitive development make it difficult for them to juggle abstractions such as writing, identity, or to integrate cultural values and customs.

As a result, their capacity to become fully actualized human beings is forever atrophied, even though they may never realize their loss. When removed from the wild, these humans often run away and go back to their "home" environments. In it, they act with an instinctive and sensory relationship to their surroundings; a quality that we might well envy, but not enough to pay its price in feral currency. [23]

This extreme example of a life path highlights to what extent behaviour and identity are not innate to us. Instead, they are assembled in the same way that a fictional character must be put together. As in a play, our social roles are formed by how we are directed, clothed, scripted, and supported by other actors and props. A stage's play and life's play differ only in their locations and durations. [24]

The unrelenting build-up of our identities and the multiple institutionalized railings that guide our upbringing are so taken for granted that we rarely consider how much our socialization is the result of massive efforts by many people, over many years, starting with our most vulnerable and unresisting state, at birth. From these early impressions on, the strongest forces around us shape us well into adulthood.

As surely as the pliable medium of moist clay allows imprints to sink in, so are we pressed into taking specific conceptual, psychological, and emotional roles. This is done in every style from care, to indifference, to abuse. Our identity is further formed from the descriptions contained in our thoughts and feelings. We tend to repeat our favourite impressions until they become part of our story, one that we present as inflexible, but actually spelled with our own pens.

Why be a prop in someone else's story when you can tell your own? *Sara Zift* [25]

The first civilized form that we get is a name: the wandering social address by which others can find us. Our name is a ticket that admits us into the world of constant objects. Without it, we have no cultural location and the first thing someone will do is give us one, if only that of a "Jane" or a "John Doe." A name, however, is only the title of our life's documentary. As with many titles, it is not unique, and as with any story, it could have been written differently; the author alone decides.[26]

When we move away from our name, we get into areas in

which we alone must orient ourselves. There is no name for the self that loves what it does, and no explanation for what seduces us; there is no way but our own to synthesize the many "I"s that we enter and exit in life.

The significance of identity's composite structure is that its parts can be shaped or removed simply by accepting or rejecting specific information. Otherwise, if we do not cultivate the information by which we live, then we are fated to act in the role that our history, environments, and cultures dictate to us.[27] That said: the advantage of being formed into an identity at birth is that we do not have to invent it from scratch. The disadvantage of this convenience, however, is that others will have defined our identity long before we can ever understand what they have done to us.

All the world's a stage,
And all the men and women merely players;
They have their exits and their entrances,
And one man in his time plays many parts,
His acts being seven ages.
William Shakespeare; As You Like It

An identity is necessary to feel fully alive, but so is its detachment in order to feel all of life. By the time we reach some kind of autonomy, we have so much life material associated with our identity that to dismiss it feels like a form of death. As a result, we cling to it and force ourselves to play out the elements of its story rather than that of our full human state of being, which is capable of so much more. We then become vested in outcomes and fearful of failures.

Worse, whenever we long to give in to our impulses we feel in conflict between what we want to do, and what we think we *should* do. Consequently, we may wrestle all our lives with what seems to be our inevitable identity, not realizing that any identity at all, even a successful one, will eventually feel constrictive if ever we want fulfillment as a human being, rather than as just a person. Yet, even an ill-fitting identity is sometimes more reassuring than a naked, nameless self.

This dilemma is minimized when we give ourselves a break from being someone specific. Rarely on our path to self-actualization is there this mandate to take time out and be no one, to just be. Such an opportunity however, is priceless. It returns us to our inner wilderness where existential natures are left to the merits of their strengths and wills. In this untamed habitat, we see that how we feel about our anonymous self is the most important factor for how to prioritize our lives .

Ironically, most of the people who deliberately set out to shed their identity's social conditioning still do so as the person that they think they are. They do not yet realize that the first thing to transcend is the idea of being someone who is in a quest for not just transcendence, but for anything.

Such an approach is not obvious for we so strongly assume the inescapability of identity that we do not think to test its limits; we wear it like a skin. Meanwhile, our authentic self is persistently trying to express its way out, sometimes to the point of explosion and crisis. Nevertheless, once we clearly see that our identity is a synthetic construction then removing it offers no more resistance than taking off our clothes. In doing so, we do not think that we cease to exist, we simply know that we are stripped down to our naked essence.

Identity, like garments, can also be slipped off. If identity were actually merged with us then no one could appropriate it out of our sight. The fact is that identity has become something to steal because data, not a body, is enough to fulfill the social requirement for being a person. Only our own authenticity of being cannot be detached from us. We are not who we are, but how we are who we are, as well as how we are not, what we are not.

The details of our way of being are what either build, or limit a connection to our roots: the crossfield of being, (or however else you wish to call the source of life itself.) The only way that this field can have authentic content about each of us is if at the more surface levels, we remain convinced as to the reality of our individual identity, and at deeper ones can overlook it and from there, realize our fundamental oneness. This viewpoint automatically catalyzes customized experiences, as if the universe were aware of us on an individual basis, which it is. The cosmos cannot help but know us all, since we are each its device for taking on unique forms.

Though the very point of our identity's function is for us to get into it fully, nonetheless, our ability to detach from it is essential for relief when this same identity is overstressed. Once detached, we can readily direct our materiality under the crossfield's influx of information, which will always guide us towards any realignment needed. Subsequently, we can "re-attach" to an identity whose well-being is now restored thanks to the relief and support offered by our temporary departure from it.

When we realize that all of being is only in this instant reduced to individual personhood—ours—then we are free to live our lives, all the while knowing that a life's essence is that of a story. As such, we can alter it through the words and images by which we process our experiences.

Absent this perspective, our summation of "I am who I am" limits what we think we should be able to know, whereas the pool of what can be known is far greater than what any identity can claim. The simple fact of being in existence offers experiences that have nothing to do with being a person. Such a transcendental consciousness is within obvious reach when we take it for granted that our identity is a fictional character and we, its most influential author.

The same process that socializes us into being somebody specific is the very one that provides us with a foothold from which to reach our freedom from it. As soon as we see our identity as the vehicle but not the driver, then our being becomes released from its constant self-remembrance, from its dedicated service to only one person. Our fulfillment is then not a question of reforming ourselves, but of temporarily putting aside our identity as the synthetic fabric that it is. Freed of the shadows that identity can cast, enlightenment is then the inevitable result of our divestment.

Any reach for an identity-free expanded consciousness will neither cause us to become disoriented nor to be socially on the fringe. On the contrary, unconditional access to all of life's information is part of our human birthright, which is to thrive and to create freely with whatever materials we find.

Paradoxically, it is when we disperse the smoke and mirrors of being someone specific that we are best at being exactly that person. The difference from before is that we see our identity as an instrument and not as the totality of our being. In symmetry with developing our identity, we can now cultivate its companion experience: a sense of unity with all of life.

9

EXPENSIVE REALITY

I become conscious of words that no one else can hear, telling me things, guiding me, evaluating my actions. I am doing something perfectly ordinary – I am thinking– and it takes the form of a voice in my head.[28]

HOW WE SPEND OUR TIME thinking is as concrete a form of debit or credit as money is. Money and freedom of thought go together: the more money we have, the less we can be forced to think when we don't feel like it. The less money we have, just the opposite is true; in that case, we are forced to think about many things whether we want to or not.

Being compelled to think means that our mind has been taken hostage by a given subject matter, one from which we won't be released until we have paid the sometimes agonizing, price of processing it through, such as: "How will I pay the x, y, or z?"

Anything that leads to undesirable thinking is a form of expense, no matter if it is a difficult relationship, a malfunctioning machine, illness, deception, poverty, etc. Forced thinking unavoidably activates our nervous system and spends our emotional and intellectual energies. It also expends our time in at least two directions: the time that it takes to think about the matter, and the time it takes to get back to a subject that we really want to think about; something that we are often too exhausted from our imposed thinking to do.

Expensive reality for the rich is a different kind of expense than it is for the poor. The expenditure of thought does not come from "if" they can get the money and "if" they can buy, but "how much more" money should they aim for, and "what exactly" to buy.

The concept of "expensive" reality is not a fanciful description; there is a direct etymological line from *expense* to *pensive*—to be in a thoughtful state.[29] Their common semantic root relates to *weight*, which leads us directly to *gravity*. Gravity, depending upon its degree, is that force which leaves us no choice but to be pulled towards something's mass . In like fashion, the greater the gravity of a matter the more we are pulled into its orbit, and unless we can resist, the more we are pushed to take it seriously. [30]

Because the word *serious* is also etymologically related to *weight*, it too brings us back to *pensive*.[31] As with a physical weight, the more serious something is, the more energy is needed to move it around. This energy can take the form of money, whereby we can afford to delegate the work to someone else, or if no money is available, in the form of thoughts on how to deal with the weighty matter.

You name it, in most industrialized societies, the acquisition of anything will either cost money or else personal energy in the form of thinking—and ultimately, in the form of feelings, even though these may remain temporarily unnoticed in the background. From this it follows that when we know how to avoid being forced to think, then we are creating a form of personal wealth.

Our thinking space is as valuable as money and even more so because money cannot buy insight, imagination, happiness, peace, inspiration, or creativity. To forego thinking for oneself is, therefore, to toss aside one of our most powerful tools for shaping a life with enough resources to meet all our needs & wants.

As it is, whenever we do not think for ourselves, it is guaranteed that others will do our thinking for us, and usually to make life easier for themselves. Not always in an exploitative way, but because the quest for self-benefit is integral to every being, and all unclaimed material is fair game.

Most of us already know how it feels when others do something at our expense. Forced to deal with those realities that have been placed at our doorstep, we pick up the tab for the lot. Meanwhile, the imposers saved themselves the expense of thinking about how to do things in a just and equitable way.

How we think reality "really" works determines if we can tell the difference between thoughts that we must consider, and those that we're sure we can ignore. Unless we spend some time filtering our thoughts, we will be living from conceptual blueprints imprinted by others. As a general guiding principle, we need to remove any concepts that limit us from transforming our reality. In the space these leave behind, we cultivate the paradigm that links our external reality to the activities of our inner one.

> *What wealth and education and prestige and a higher station in life gives you is the freedom to focus on the self.* [32]

When these inner doors open to our potential for materializing our needs independently of external circumstances, we create wealth from the inside out. We can now think for ourselves in the way that materially wealthy people do. No longer does our thinking need to be based upon a defensive and all-around preparedness; instead, its work becomes one of planting and refining conceptual seeds related to our needs and hopes.

It is not only that this process cultivates our nervous system to align itself in anticipation, but thoughts themselves also attract their contents such that needed circumstances and objects come to meet us halfway. The more we can think on a goal before we act on its behalf, the fewer the actions we will have to take, while those that we do take will be particularly to the point.

Making use of our inner realm in this way gives us a chance to both think and feel deeply. It gives us a space from which to draw out what we need from an unobstructed connection to our source of creativity: the crossfield of being, as I call it. This crossfield takes the emotionally fueled energy of our imagination and instructs us into those actions necessary for our successes.[33]

What draws money is the will to do so. Many people do not let this process flow into fruition because they first assess if they deserve to be happy and fullfilled. This way of being is below that of even the most primitive organism. It cannot be pointed out often enough: from the cells on up, every other living being unapologetically rallies all possible resources to satisfy itself.

They can afford this attitude because they are organic, not synthetic beings. Only humans pre-condition their happiness, often without realizing it or why. This way of being is very expensive indeed; it sets up one thought against another on a battlefield within. The most cost-effective route in life is to cultivate our own authenticity—the needed resources will then follow.

To claim our world of thoughts is to liberate ourselves to think as we wish, a process that is closer to improvisation than it is to a set score. As with some forms of music, you don't necessarily know where the next note will be, but if you keep playing, the beats naturally progress into a thrilling and rhythmical arrangement. Freethinking is the same: each thought finds its way towards the next one until there is a totality of insight involving a composed worldview. To maintain this tonal play is the goal of most wealthy people.

Released from the bonds of regular labour and commanding enough resources to materialize the products of one's imagination, the wealthy person can live the profoundest life of all, with two pitfalls. One is at whose expense is this wealth acquired? When wealth is obtained in an exploitative and corrupt way then it cannot offer the ease of conscience that is needed to truly enjoy life. Instead, it becomes a means of escape and entrenchment.

And the other is how the appetites of our physicality and emotional needs will tempt us into a balancing act between having enough luxury to satisfyingly engage our senses, and having so much that we become spoiled—like fruit.

With either of these pitfalls we become imperceptibly possessed by the needs of our own possessions and at ever-greater costs to our inner freedom, we begin to serve what once served us. However, when both kinds of resources are cultivated, the inner and the outer, then our external wealth will not undermine our inner one, but expand it instead.

10

M / Honey

"Somebody's got to live this life," he says, gesturing to the pristine view from his penthouse villa.[34]

Money illustrates how organic beings need fresh fuel to continue living. The form that this fuel *must* take depends upon a creature's physicality. Even if a dog were to eat it, money alone would not ensure its survival: all non-human animals must get their energy directly from the food chain. Most human beings, however, cannot avoid placing money between their stomachs and the food that they eat. Even more, humans use money to feed not only their biology, but also their psychology.

Money is accurately called a "currency" because like electricity, it causes raw energy to flow such that we trade what we do for money, and trade money for what others do. We're used to thinking that money buys things, but things also buy money. Regardless of what it is, a business acquires our money in exchange for what it offers. Before we can sell our money however, we first need to have it.

The possession of money takes several paths whose characters are illustrated by how each is named. This is worth noticing because every verbal framework carries with it certain implications of control between the person and their financial reality. We may say that we "work" somewhere, "earn a living," or that we "make a living." We rarely say that we "create a life" as a way to illustrate that we see money finding its way to us, rather than our having to seek it out.

In whatever way we generate our money right now, it's most empowering to see it as simply one of several steps towards a financially independent life, one where we have the ability to create from our desire and will to do so. Otherwise, to think along any other terms is to limit our options. For example: to think in terms of having "to work" says it in a direct way: what we do is not necessarily fun but certainly labour. To "earn a living" also implies an element of hard work, including the implication that survival, and therefore life, is not a given but something that must be well,...earned.

A less burdensome view than the concepts of "work" or of "earning a living" is the one termed "making a living." Within this frame, there is no initial implication of having to prove the merits of our existence (by earning it) or of labour (by working), but we still must be able to gather and combine the elements needed to "make" the intended assets and support systems.

Because it implies greater self-rule, to "make a living" is the beginning of an enterprising approach, one that leads to more options than those involved in the concepts of either working, or of earning a living. The creative aspect of the "making" element also has the added factor of an internal process that coaches us towards our goals. The limitations inherent in making anything, however, is that it still looks outwardly to gather its raw materials—since you can't "make" anything without the requisite resources. This relationship to money still thinks in terms of limits set by external circumstances and sources.

All of the above styles of economic sufficiency lead to survival if we succeed, or else to fatal decline if we do not—with many shades of insufficiency in between. The hard-core character of these models assume that we must get everything from outside of ourselves, that we are left to our lone skills for resources, and that we are in competition with others—and perhaps even with our own goals and yearnings. These zero-sum games are an unsophisticated template at best and, at worst, a form of socially supported violence.

The most liberated form of acquiring money is to "create" our life's necessities and luxuries from the inside out by a process of attraction. Long before it gathers external things, thinking that we can create our life starts by rallying our imagination and its ideal outcomes. The more we cultivate this practice, the more the outside aligns itself in kind. We already start to feel wealthier as soon as we embrace the concept that we can achieve prosperity from within ourselves.

The conceptual framework of "creating" our life rather than earning it or making it, catalyzes our inner world into a co-creative collaboration with the universe at large. This collaboration assists us in achieving any lifestyle goals, the details of which are frequently updated from the feedback of our feelings and of our evolving intentions.

Comfortable lunching with top-tier collectors like the producer David Geffen and the heiress Joan Tisch, buyers who would not blanch at the thought of plunking down a few million for a painting.[35]

The intensity of our desire to reach our goals will determine the strength of the neurological commitment that we are pledging towards our own potential—a pledge whose power is matched by life itself. This is not wishful thinking, but a form of psychosomatic manifestation. To the degree that our heart and mind vow to further our ideals, to that extent we have our connection to the universal mind's ability to help us reach them.

"Money is no object..." Just savour that phrase and hear what it is saying. When we view money as an object outside of ourselves, then we must seek it on its own terms. However, when we view money as a reflection of our personal energy, then it is virtually already in our own hands to be increased.

In furtherance of our prosperity, we need to employ our inner world as a workshop from where we envision the life that we want and need. This involves deliberately landscaping our feelings and thoughts away from any competing scenarios that flesh out our insecurities. Instead, we shape thoughts and feelings towards an affirmation of our power to direct the quality and contents of our lives.

Until we're able to do so however, we're faced with the facts of our lacking resources and any affirmations may feel like mere wishful thinking. To get around the cold facts of "what is" we need a technique that gives us a concrete truth about our desired goal.

For this we simply need to connect to how our heart will feel when that goal is reached. Our imagination will readily do that work for us as we visualize expressing our happiness or relief at the wished for event happening: "I'm so glad that x, y, z, is paid; it's such a relief that x, y, z, is solved. This technique also works in helping others: "I'm really happy that you x, y, z...."

We don't need to figure out how the desired changes will come, nor whether we can do what it takes. Instead, we connect with the desired reality in a true state in which *it already exists*: namely our anticipated joy and relief when it arrives. This technique is especially useful with very challenging situations.

Whether we now have challenges or not, health is the first form of money that we can give ourselves because we then use it to acquire other forms of wealth. Whenever the thought of money comes to mind, first refer to your state of energy—whether emotional, mental, physical, or spiritual—and to the extent that you can, consistently address any needs for either its restoration, or its maintenance.

When we neglect our health, we are creating an ongoing tax on our energy and our moods. Even if our health is not now what we want it to be, we can still begin to address whatever is in our means to foster its well-being, one small step at a time.

By taking care of our biology's various systems, we create a clear passageway for life to provide for the rest of our needs through the flow of information that it can now deliver to us. This will arrive in various forms, from ideas, to prompts for action, to "lucky breaks," to chance encounters.

Regardless of the image of money as something rooted in evil, there is no inherent harm in the desire to be wealthy in terms of money. Much of the exquisite workmanship that some long to do could not be done if there were no customers to purchase it. The crucial question is: at whose expense—if anyone's—does our wealth come into being?

The process attached to what we own, and to how we were able to acquire it, inevitably influences the quality of our energy. The more we have a peaceful conscience regarding what we buy and how we are bought, the more smoothly can energy flow through us, clearly and without interference or reversals. [36]

The cleaner that energy is, the more we find that our life experiences and resources easily align with our needs and wants. As a result, we become less concerned with the linear accumulation of what we think we *should* have to be happy. Instead, we prioritize staying true to our authentic self, which always senses and knows what will actually be fulfilling in the long run. The outcome is that our customized life will put itself together as swiftly as our emotions can accommodate it. We can trust this process even if the way and timing to our successes are different from what we expected.

11

EGOS EVERYWHERE I GO

THE REDUCTION OF ONE'S EGO is commonly, though wrongly, urged for spiritual self-improvement. Having an ego is by itself not a problem, because only its character determines if it is harmful to self or others. Rather, egos are necessary engines and in connection with humans, highly effective facilitators in the pursuit of ideals.

We would cultivate neither understanding nor compassion if we did not recognize these qualities' valuable egos and wish to add them to our own. The troublemaker in our ego's character is more likely to be our self-image and the lengths that we will go to protect it from our own criticism and that of others.

Accusing our personal ego as the spoiler in our efforts for transcendence &/or spirituality, only comes from the success of the ego of the "non-ego." To take a position against having an ego itself has an ego—and a rather large one at that. Whereas an individual ego asserts: "I am" in association with something specific, a non-ego endlessly asserts "I am not that, nor that, nor that," ad infinitum.

In effect, the size of the non-ego increases with each ego that it is not. Since, regardless of context, it denies the concept of ego itself, a non-ego has a virtual infinity of material with which to associate itself by disassociation.

Not only can we embrace having a personal ego, but we will also need it as a guide towards our objectives. Without egos, nothing would have enough self-assertion to persist with its existence; there would be no motions and so, no change.

An ego motivates a being to be what it is and, especially, to strive to be even more of itself. Egos are not limited to people; they exist in every creation, be it animal, object, situation, feeling, concept, idea, person, and whatever else you can name. To the extent that it can, a being's ego acts with all its resources to maintain or, better yet, to increase its status. This egotistic thrust of desire to "thrive in the game" is inseparable from any existence. The differences between egos simply come from what tools each one has to achieve its ambitious expansion.

Some things have a very sizable and long-term ego by what they are (vital resources, cultural traditions, the "classics") while others have a short-lived ego because it was artificially enlarged to begin with (a fad).

An ego not only applies to a thing's overall being, but also to the separate parts that comprise it, each of which has its own specific and dedicated ego enfolded within the larger one of the whole. In some circumstances, a part's ego gets to increase its own status in equal measure to the ego of its overall container. For example, olive oil has a life of its own and, arguably, as big an ego as the olives themselves. Just think back at how often you've bought whole olives versus how often you've bought olive oil.

No matter what ego we consider, its chances for success can be greatly enhanced—as in the case of olive oil—through a host, such as humans. We make very good ones because we layer sociocultural egos over each thing's native ones, and so increase its total ego. The mathematics of egos can also involve subtraction whereby, although something's ego has value in the long run, it is nonetheless minimized in the short term—the denial of the need for a healthy ecological environment, for example.

The degree of power that something's ego has over us comes from a combination of its own properties (as with oxygen, gold) and the collective egos of the ideas that we then associate with it (gold jewelry as a status symbol, air as clean or polluted.) The social egos of each thing vary according to how they are evaluated, and by whom; this is especially true when egos of commercial value are layered over a given being's more modest native ego.

This is the case with many art objects, whose materials have a naturally small ego compared to that of their market value's ego. An etching by Rembrandt is only paper and ink; a painting by Picasso is only canvas and (possibly, house) paint. Most do not want these objects solely for their objective value, but to add their cultural egos to their own, especially that of an art work in its original form.

We may not even like the subject shown, but the ego of a high-priced original will pull us in. Consider that the social ego of an actual Van Gogh painting is far greater than that of any print of it, no matter how excellently reproduced.

If however, we are unaware of Van Gogh's reputation, then we can only value an original based on its material actuality such as how much it pleases us, if it matches the decor, or if we enjoy cypress trees. Or we might simply dislike it and throw it into the bin (the fate of more than a few thrift store purchases whose commercial value went unrecognized).[37]

We're used to associating egos only with people because they have far more options for asserting theirs than, say, a piece of paper. Its ego is passively submissive to the egos of many other forces that humans can bring to it: crumbling, water, cutting, fire, etc. That is unless it benefits from the protection of a social ego layered over it, as when the paper is money.

Egos occur in shells like Russian dolls as larger egos incorporate smaller ones: universal, planetary, national, state, organizational, family, peer group, self, inner self, transcendental self, and any number of subdivisions within each category. According to the context, the ego of the shell with the most survival and/or face-saving value is served at the expense of other egos.

Our own primary ego is composed of a cluster of egos around which the ego of our self-image wraps itself. These subdirectory egos include such aspects as temperament, mental acuity, profession, emotional intelligence, physical abilities, education, experience, connections, ownership, and so on.

The priorities for each person vary according to which ego is at play. It is not that any particular ego disappears, but rather that its advantages change according to circumstances. The leverage of a person's ego at work is not the same as when they are parents at home, out with a friend, or reading a book.

We perceive a person's ego according to the contexts in which we meet them. Due to the spellbinding nature of circumstantial egos, we may not notice the true character of another's core ego unless we know them better. Someone with an impoverished background may have very strong ego for personal refinement and for career accomplishment, but the superficial ego of their socio-economic status may make it harder for many to recognize this individual's drive and high quality.

Conversely, trust-fund babies may be seen as having important egos due to their easy access to resources, but they may actually have very weak personal ones for lack of conditions that let them prove their ego's characters and abilities to themselves and to others.

Even with a slew of options at our disposal for empowering our many egos, those of humans often require many validations from self and others before they are free to actualize in full. In stark contrast, the egos of non-humans assert themselves unconditionally, without apology, and in full accordance with the material strengths of their constituent "I am." Organic egos will not settle for less than what they can get from either their environments or from themselves.

You will rarely see a wild animal not act as it wants. So much so that, when people have supremacy over animals it is by means of the humanly created egos of tools that can dominate the egos of otherwise stronger creatures. The ego of the cattle prod is greater than the cows' ego to stay in one place; the ego of a tranquilizer will reduce an elephant's alert ego to a silent heap. The egos of bacteria, however, are as great (if not greater) than those of humans. Rather than succumb to the ego of antibiotics, their vitality becomes stronger still, to the point that many major synthetic antibiotics are now ineffective.

As a general principle, an ego will continue asserting itself until someone, or something, applies its own ego and establishes a different hierarchy.

In contrast, humans impose conditions and tests of meritocracy on their egos' needs and wants. They do so as a result of cultural forces that for many centuries have split the formulation of a human into conflicting ego camps: spiritual states versus physical ones. This division into polarized egos reduces the ego of our own spontaneous actions for fear of which character's ego will then be on the rise: the ego of being "good," and so spiritual, or that of being "bad" and so, ruled by various unsanctioned appetites.[38]

Death presents journalists with another dangerous temptation – the egomaniacal urge to link your life to the deceased's, however tenuous the connection might be.[39]

The ego of identification has a lot of choices and can merge with many other egos. For example, we eagerly identify with the egos of luxuries and seek to possess them so as to add their egos to our own. Not everyone is aware of an ego's range within an object. To some, a rock's ego is insignificant and even to be avoided because it offers a harsh contact. To a geologist, however, a rock's ego is a complex and ongoing process made of multiple egos, i.e., those of time, chemistry, weather, minerals, plant life, and others. By being in the right place at the right time, a fortunate rock enhances its ego through the informational material it can offer to its researcher, whose own ego as an expert increases in the process. Through this mutually egocentric relationship, the egos of each are augmented.

You may think that the word "ego" is just another word for "nature." This last word is too vague however, because it does not underline how the parts of something have their own ambitions for self-expansion, regardless of their current contributory role. This dynamic is due to the equal status of all things at their origin as a concept.

A concept is a form of kingdom governed by the ruler of its subject matter. In this case, the ruler consists of seed information whose nurture and consequent growth can lead to the material fulfillment of a given concept. As long as they have the leverage to do so, adept rulers can take over territories that are far greater than their own. In like fashion, something's enfolded ego can quietly assume ever-greater status and eventually, dominate. Left unchecked, these egos can turn an original intention into its opposite.

Tomatoes, for instance, whose mass transportation was first intended to bring fresh and, therefore, flavourful tomatoes to faraway stores. The rough egos of the shipping process however, bruised many of the tomatoes skins' tender egos. Rather than accept the more costly solution of increasing the ego of the packaging's protection, the choice made was to toughen the ego of the skins.

This led to gassing unripe, but harder, green tomatoes in transport so that they would turn red in transit. However, the skins' new hardiness sacrificed the tomatoes' taste, the ego of which was the original idea for transporting them. In combination with the ego of profit, the ego of hardy transportation trumped and flipped the ego of flavourful tomatoes. [40A]

Our human abilities to move, manipulate, extract, combine, and play, lead to the creation of new being-objects. In the process, egos may well increase, be transformed, or else disappear. They do so according to this general principle: creativity combined with culture increases the specificity of objects and the number of their egos.

Forks, for example, which originally emerged to refine the fingers' collective egos of lifting food to the mouth. From the ego of basic forks came: fish forks, fruit forks, salad forks, serving forks, and a multitude of other forks. These are all extensions of what fingers used to do. As the egos of the concept of forks ascended, that of fingers for eating was reduced.

We can more effectively reach our own egos' goals when we are prepared for the abundance of self-assertive egos that surround us. As a result, we can understand that our motivations may not primarily be originating from our own ego after all. They may arise instead, from the influence of something's ego upon us in the service of its own expansion. We then realize that not everything has to be permitted into being, no matter how seductive the call.

I would prefer to have invented a machine that people could use and that would help farmers with their work–for example a lawnmower. Mikhail Kalashnikov, Inventor of the AK47 rifle [40-b]

If you define ethics as a commitment not to devalue anyone's life by what you do, then the ethical challenge is to sometimes refrain from a creation, and to not let an ego assert itself through us. We might then need to refuse to midwife into life that which will become its enemy. An ongoing awareness of our shared substrate as a single being can dissolve the conflicting activities of any egos and modifies them to accommodate those of others, but without demoting any one of them.

In both the short and the long run, our state of being is not in competition with other beings but in collaboration with them. The submission of one's own ego for the wellbeing of a mutually nourishing one is the basis for much needed planetary harmony.

Because universal forces will not arbitrarily favour one ego over another, this ideal needs to develop and increase an ego of its own. It does not matter to life what humans create or what egos will come into and out of being; only we have to care.

Further, the more we want to fulfill our potential, the more flexible and adaptable our egos must be. In today's complex world, we increasingly need to cultivate the ego of being in the moment, along with our capacity to let go of it. Otherwise, the unchanging ego of a fixed cultural identity traps us into a storyline whose ego we believe to be the whole of "me". Such a bonding forces us into a tight oscillation between either our acceptance, or our rejection of it. This causes us to lose our natural relationship with the various egos that inevitably arise during an authentic life; egos that can either be our allies or our obstacles.

12

Consciousness as Sensory Information

Not just humans, but all beings interact with their environments such that they can accurately be said to be conscious. To be conscious represents being one with the knowledge of something; what each is conscious of and in what way, depends upon the form of its existence.[41]

Through its cells, a comparatively simple being such as a leaf is conscious of—has sensory information about—light and water. It draws these elements into itself according to its cells' states of health. A rock is also conscious, just in a simpler way than a leaf. When a sufficient force strikes a rock, its molecules receive the sensory information of that object's supremacy, and the rock cleaves apart.

The rock and the leaf are always in the Now and act upon their sensory information for the sake of any optimal outcomes to the extent that circumstances allow. There is not one healthy leaf on the planet that can willfully *decide* not to respond to light, or not to absorb available nutrients, nor rock that will decide not to break when subjected to a sufficient force.

Humans, however, can abandon information and disregard it altogether, with better or worse consequences. Ironically, the first information ignored is usually the one that gets the last word: our physicality's sensory experiences, which often get pushed to the breaking point as people try to live up to socially created expectations.

Modern life's intense levels of abstraction make it easy to ignore that being alive is always based on various degrees of concrete physicality. Not just outer events, but also all inner ones. Though intangible, a thought, an imagination, a feeling, a memory, each is experienced through the materiality of 4-Dimensional chemical and neurological processes. When our physicality breaks down we die to this life, as all things do.

As such, our biology's prime duty is to balance its own processes. The body's innate intelligence goes beyond simply managing its cellular activities; it also engages in correcting psychological, emotional, and intellectual imbalances. Furthermore, our body receives existential information that seeks its definition from the deepest levels of our being. It is from these communication centers that we get hunches, premonitions, and gut feelings–even dreams. The more we act upon them, the more readily they manifest.

Our physical survival (and by extension, that of our property,) is always our main priority. In this respect, we are zero degrees of separation from every other living creature. For all our social complexities and mastery of materials, our body's sensory requirements have not changed from our animal origins. What *has* changed is our relationship to them.

In various ways, both Eastern and Western religions have downgraded our physicality as the less worthy of our assets. Its flesh and basic appetites are contrasted with the light touch that spiritual practices are reputed to offer. Consequently, the body's needs and any efforts at fulfilling them are viewed as superficial, misguided pursuits.

Physicality's undeserved bad press, however, only comes from the success of spirituality's ego. The more it downgrades physicality, the more spirit elevates itself. Because of this highly successful self-promotion, those who seek a more sublime life turn their efforts towards taking care of their spirit, which is fine, but at the expense of their sensory information, which is not.

The exact opposite should take place. We need to care for

our body in order to fulfill our spiritual ideals, which ironically, are always about an improved physical experience at some level or other, and not about a sensation-less disembodied state. Even heaven is supposed to feel like something emotionally pleasant.

Our body is the fundamental wilderness from which we are inseparable. Its need for sunlight, air, water, nutrients, and shelter keep us subliminally directed towards sensory physicality in all their various forms. Even more, our body's state of wellbeing determines what sensory information we can receive and how well we interpret it.

In contrast, our body's unjust demotion and the back-burner prioritization of its needs, blunts and deforms our sensory experiences. Due to this neglect, we inevitably experience a reduced quality of being, distortions of perception, and a compensatory fantasy life. The consequence is that we lose empathy, perspective, and a sense of direction for where our long-term wellbeing can be found. We then live within condensed emotional parameters and so cannot "feel" well. Conversely, acknowledging our body's requirements grounds us at very deep levels and, simultaneously, keeps us from living on purely abstract ones.

From this point of view, it is shortsighted to take our body's health for granted and to give it attention only when it begins to falter. This care-by-crisis attitude comes from misunderstanding the body's role as an interface between our imaginations and the materializations that we experience. Such an oversight is encouraged through the contents of media and their seductive manipulation of our imagination.

Be it for entertainment, education, or as various shades of news, media's technology seduces and distorts us away from full physical experiences, even as it offers them in virtual forms. The readiness with which our consciousness can participate in any subject matter through imagination and spectatorship alone, encourages our thirst for sensory stimulation without ever being able to quench it. There is no way that a virtual product ever can; its maximum capacity of 3-Dimensionality lacks the full weight of a given 4-Dimensional reality and how it tests our nervous system in real time.

This was not always the case. Before massive media, each person had a comparatively unique life of imagination that was populated with images and sounds differently composed from everyone else's. In contrast, today's viewing of mass broadcasts means that multitudes of people are fed the exact same text and images to digest, and in many cases, simultaneously.

It is no exaggeration then, to say that millions of unique imaginations have been replaced by variations on a single one, itself the product of only a handful of minds. What we now see is no longer where we are, but where someone else has placed us. Unavoidably, our system tries on all of these different virtual realities via its mirror neurons. These, as we know, activate in partially the same way as if the observed matter were happening in full dimensionality—except that these neurons can only offer up to 3 of the 4 dimensions that they depict.

A little learning is a dangerous thing;
Drink deep, or taste not the Pierian spring;
There shallow draughts intoxicate the brain,
And drinking largely sobers us again. [42]

This spectator phenomenon has its place, but when mirror neurons must metabolize depictions of violence, disaster, or exclusive ultra-rich lifestyles, then the nervous system gets stimulated without the means to experience a 4-Dimensional process of context, development, and consequences. Moreover, since the on-screen stories are compressed, we artificially experience in minutes what it would take hours, days, years, to actually live through. What is complete information on a screen therefore, becomes ignorance and untruths away from it.

The residual effect is that virtuality in excess reduces our abilities to orient ourselves, and to accurately perceive what is happening right in front of us. Due to our lean record of accomplishments in 4-dimensions, we increasingly function within an atrophied range of actions, reactions, abilities, and self-assessments. Meanwhile, only a life that contains all degrees of functionality throughout all the 4 dimensions can educate us to act self-confidently within it.

The great irony is that references for all subject matter on-screen are experiences of full interaction with the physical forms to which they point. Meanwhile, our own experience becomes limited to getting a snack and something to drink while we sit and watch a screen. In the background, the credibility of words & images rests on the fact that we subliminally understand that life always imposes upon us its full sensory dimensionality, and thereby causes us to experience sensations of one kind or another.

> *It's one thing when you watch things on TV or in a movie, but it's totally different when you see someone you knew personally.* [43]

What we sense always begins any experience. We acknowledge this with our insistence that things should "make sense" and with our rejection of "non-sense." These criteria are only pragmatic. No matter how sophisticated the situation, sensing's information always starts with the basics of action: do we come closer or go farther away? Do we go fast or slow? Do we contract or expand? Are we attracted, repulsed, or left indifferent?

These are the same sensory questions that any sentient being constructs on an ongoing basis, including birds, snakes, insects, amoeba, cells, molecules, atoms, and quarks. To be unable to practice these direct kinds of responses atrophies our self-knowledge and consequently, our knowledge on where we fit within life.

This is an especially poignant fact if we've ignored signs of our physicality's imbalances and then they force us to deal with all 4 dimensions on their own terms. At that point, all that matters, and at any price, is our health—which money alone cannot always buy. When its status is fully appreciated, however, our body can be trusted to exercise its innate intelligence for healing. To enable this activation, we need to accept the vital nature of all the dimensions that comprise the experience of being alive.

As our relationship to our body becomes one of care-taking, then we no longer impose upon it our own psychosocial images. Instead, we become free to sense our being's prompts as they guide us to provide for its needs, which ultimately are also our own. And, eventually, our neurology will reflect to us optimal self-actualization, the fullness of which we may never have known before.

Not our ideas about how we are, but our deepest neurological activity is that which is "really" real about us as individuals. In all cases, and at any moment, we can foster into existence "the real me" in full actualization of its expressive and creative energies. "Me's" changing forms and contents thus become one constantly evolving stream-of-being whose parts interflow unconditionally.

In its fully actualized state, what is real does not cancel its foundation as pure energy. On the contrary, the structural quality of our conceptual energy is exactly what determines the seemingly firm realities we all get to face. As a result, we are neither fully tested nor completely validated until our longed-for experiences manifest into their physical forms.

We have an appreciative audience of at least one when we sing in the shower, but the feeling is far more stunning, and the demands on our nervous system far more taxing, when we perform before thousands. Whether we really want the more intense version or remain satisfied with the basic one is for each to know.

Unique beings that we are, it is up to us to understand our own natures and plans clearly enough to direct and guide their vitality into actualization. We attain this knowledge by being one with our physical self. The more self-actualized individuals there are in life, the better it is for all. For any one of us to remain unfullfilled degrades the entire world, whereas our health and joys can only uplift it.

•

13

Love, Tell Me More...

Of all forms of caution, caution in love is perhaps the most fatal to true happiness. Bertrand Russell [44]

The sensation of being in love feels so wonderfully ecstatic that it rarely occurs to us that love's effects come from wanting more information—of all kinds—about the beloved. Without hesitation, love avidly reaches for the next interaction in order to receive evermore information in all possible forms: sights, smells, tastes, touches, fantasies, sounds, plans. Our splendid love-based emotions come from our desire to sensorily experience increasing aspects of whom or what we love.

With hardly any hesitation, the ardent lover will take on challenges and obstacles to increase their informational content regarding the love object, and opportunities to do so are sought out, if not forced into being to the point of obsession.

Paradoxically then, love is not first about the beloved, but about how our love for them affects us. Love feels as it does because, by unconditionally accepting all information, our being cannot help but expand beyond its usual limits. In love, we are released into new self-experiences and surprising ways of perceiving and living life.

To love and to feel loved inspires a thirst in us for more of our own authenticity. As we act to our optimal capacities and incorporate life's offerings into a fresh wide-open self, this dynamic leads to liberation, relief, extension, purpose, and to a great surge of energy. Our self-reinvention then activates the latent potential that we've always had on our own but were not sufficiently catalyzed or inspired to actualize.

In romantic love, we see ourselves freshly empowered through the eyes of the other, and consequently, we no longer wish to safeguard the boundaries of our personal self. Instead, we offer an enormous degree of trust and remove from our nervous system many former protections against potential risks, and we now see our openness as opportunity rather than vulnerability. As a result, we are finally freed from our own self-imposed limitations of identity and its insecurities. We are thus able to feel the fullness of our experiences in the Now and encouraged to expand our self-definition.

It is this promising and pulsating rhythm of unrestrained expansion and contraction, of the systolic and diastolic pulse of a universe stretching out all around us that contributes to love's intoxicating effects. We both inspire and are inspired. In extreme cases, everything but information about the love object, is immaterial. To be "in love" is that ultimate state in which we are fully surrounded and acted upon by love's heartbeat; we take it as our own. Thus coupled, our heart becomes the hub that receives experiences of the beloved through all the channels accessible.

Nothing is too much to do or to go through for the sake of our love. We feel no pain in the sense of boundaries overstepped: their dissolution does not activate any defenses in us. We are willingly open to greater reception as we invite entry of the beloved's information into all parts of our being. This is why tokens of love have such power. Anything that can be associated with the love object becomes a way to experience them.

As with fireworks, the trajectories of our emotions come in many styles, but the dynamic of latent potential released and its exciting effects is true for all. A person's stimulated state matches the motions of an electron following excitation from a source—heat in the case of an electron, and a beloved in the case of a person. In both instances, the external stimulus causes the electron/person to move to a higher level of energy. As each falls back to their less excited state, they release the energy of that higher one and throw off a spark. This literally becomes light in a lamp, and in a lover it turns into heartfelt action, effort, self-sacrifice, stars in the eyes.

When love is requited, the synergy of self-expansion goes both ways. The feelings of each person are vastly increased according to the lengths that their unified selves are willing to go to receive ever more information about one another.

My Beloved Brontosaurus: On the road with old bones, new science, and our favorite dinosaurs.
Brian Switek [45]

Romantic love is not the only self-actualizing catalyst of love available to us, for our being can be made to expand through a variety of loves. The territory of each will differ according to which systems within us are activated: emotional, intellectual, spiritual, physical, or any combination of these. To love a subject matter also triggers a similar release and self-expansion into unconditional sensory information. This kind of love welcomes any opportunity to increase the knowledge of what it loves: a field of study, a profession, a place, cats, (dogs too...), you name it.

The love between a person and a subject of interest usually leads to willing self-sacrifice of one's own personal neurological spaces. Examples abound of how devotion to a subject matter adds to our knowledge about it, but not about its researcher beyond their name. In many instances, that name becomes associated with significant discoveries related to the subject as if it were the love child of this union. This is common in the hard sciences, where we talk about Planck's constant, or Newtonian physics, for example.

On the subject of children, most parents come to love theirs by the very frequency of varied informational encounters, and by the natural parental role of providing the most basic information to their offspring. This mutual reverberation of information between parent and child amplifies the emotions already biologically associated with parental love. The inevitable lack of boundaries during early care-taking builds up a library of sensory information about a child that no one else can ever have about them.

More than that, a parent's role is to select and increase their child's informational database from their own. Over many years, this leads to a shared pool of information and by default, becomes a form of platonic intimacy. This informational give and take creates a kind of love that is unlike any other. Unless we are obsessed with them, we will not need or want to know that much about anyone. That is, until we are forced to absorb information as caretakers of parents, in which case a reversal of informational roles takes place.

Whether we are loved or not can readily be determined by the degree to which another welcomes the sharing of our information. Equally, our capacity to love another person is measured by the degree to which we unconditionally receive informational content about them. Receptivity to another's contents of consciousness is essential for us to know how to care for the loved-one on their own terms.

When someone says that they love, but resist taking on additional information about the supposed beloved, then either, they may not love enough, or they might fear intimacy. This fear is the anxiety of being forced into emotional receptivity. In other words: fear of losing control over the sensory information that one must process.

Intimacy is itself no guarantee of permanent closeness. One of the reasons why once loving relationships disintegrate past a certain point comes from getting to know more than we can neurologically integrate. In the course of a once romantic cohabitation, the subject matters that we end up having information about is sometimes quite different from what we found attractive or were shown during the courting phase.

When living in close quarters we have no choice but to be privy to knowledge about the other's finances, the shortcomings of their lifestyle, their history, worries, character under stress, health issues, etc. Consequently, the uncomfortable internal states that we experience from some aspects of this new information can spill over into our formerly successful interactions. We have now fallen out of love and into default intimacy.

Along that road, couples who separate often stop wanting to take in more information about one another. Their nervous system withdraws from having to factor in any favourable data. To the degree that there is an absence of love, you can be sure that there is also a corresponding degree of contraction away from new information. Hate, in fact, is ardent resistance to any favourable information about a given subject.

When we hate, we actively reject and shrink away from knowing more than we already do—which may not be much in the case of prejudices. We also seek to negate any validating content about something hated so as not to let our nervous system inadvertently hyperlink into any favourable assessments of it. We contract rather than expand. By inference, social or personal conditions that foster contraction, such as poverty, are going to limit one's capacity to love and likely engender hate besides.

While in love, our receptivity to information can cease at any point where the content becomes genuinely distasteful or contrary to values whose transgression degrades our self-image. At that point, we resist additional information about the other and revise what information we already have. This may not be easy to do, for we have already let down our neurological guard and it takes time to desensitize our nerves from further influxes of information.

Those who nonetheless, keep taking in troublesome information about the other, either love them unconditionally or are addicted to them. A mother emotionally shelters her criminally violent son, a lover adapts to the other's dysfunction and becomes dysfunctional themselves. Either scenario is based on love because it keeps accepting information even when it leads to suffering. It may not be healthy, but it is love nonetheless, a dark intimacy.

And she said, "I think you love her, you just don't like her."
I thought about what she said for a second and realized, yep, I dislike almost everything about her and if we weren't married, I would never associate with someone like that.[46]

Intimacy is a question of kind and degree. People who grow up in a shared household have it either by preference, or by default. Due to architectural constraints and to the inevitable statistics of frequent encounters under a variety of circumstances, household members obtain unsolicited information about one another's personal spaces: a bathroom door is left unlocked, one comes to breakfast without grooming, phone conversations are overheard, incompetence is unedited, and so on.

The difference between love and default intimacy is that, in the former we willingly reach for information, but with the latter we cannot avoid it. Not all intimacy is therefore voluntary, nor is it an aspect of emotional love. Neither does all intimacy result in liking someone, even when there is love.

Not to distinguish between information gained from forced interactions and that gained from a willing reach for it, leads to the false belief that all family members must like one another. This is unrealistic; a nervous system cannot be forced to like anything or anyone, because liking is a different kind of resonance from love. We like what is like us–compatibility of neurology–but we may love what is completely different.[47]

"Angry (but true) things were said on all sides. Essentially, we all realized that for years we've been pretending we're a very close family while we all actually hate each other." [48]

As described further on, right relationship is a question of right distance.[49] Distance determines how much information is possible and how powerfully it can be delivered. With further distance, our neurological input is naturally reduced. This results in having greater inner space, which then lets us be in touch with feelings that, in fact, may be favourable towards the other under the right circumstances, i.e. the right distance. When a forced proximity comes to an end, what was once irritating can inspire a kind of retrospective acceptance, if not fondness–as when people die or move away.

Whatever the limits that we set for how much information we can comfortably accept is not the measure of our unwillingness to love, but an expression of what our nervous system can handle. We can only love as much as we can receive certain kinds of information. People have to determine their own limits and recognize when they can assimilate nothing further.

Otherwise, when we love someone to the point of self-neglect, then we are receiving excessive information about them and not enough about ourselves. Too much self-sacrifice also means that there will certainly be an upheaval and vacuum if we are left behind, such as when a child becomes adult, or a companion leaves by death, or divorce. As information about the other ends, we may experience a great emptiness that can only be filled by increasing self-knowledge–which is inevitable if we do the work of letting go.

By implication, the paradigm of love as information means that to love ourselves is to be open to all information on the subject of "me" regardless of what we may find out. Again, this is a question of including all information without resistance to it.

To unreservedly face any fact about ourselves, and at any given moment, is to love ourselves even if we do not like what we find out. By accepting information regarding the dark and the light in us, we are letting what is neurologically true trigger inevitable self-understanding. At the same time, whatever we do not like will naturally find its own resolution. Because life is a self-repairing system, it will automatically do so when we let information flow via its own play of forces.

It is only by getting to know ourselves that we can become whole and healed. We do not need to worry about what "news" we might find because our neurology constantly registered what was actually going on inside us, anyway. The text that we come to read about ourselves was always echoed as tonal textures at the level of indirect consciousness, and we regularly received this information, for example, through our reactions, our dreams. Within them, our neurology recreates the images and story lines of what we are subliminally telling ourselves all along about life and about our position within it.

Once we expand our consciousness to include updated self-information, then we will inevitably feel completely loved not only by ourselves, but also by life, and even by others. To practice love (receive information) under as many circumstances as possible is the optimal attitude for a full life. It is the only state that encourages expansion into Now's informational contents, including its relevance to the achievement of our goals.

By perceiving and acting with love, we are in our most expanded state–one that offers us the fullest range of understanding and harmony within any given interaction. It does so because to love is to reach beyond ideas about our own selves and to go into the actuality of our lives. This content will always merge into unity at our deepest levels.

All that we require and desire can come to us through the mechanism of life's full assimilation of information about us–its love for us. We can access this love directly from our inner world and do so without preconditions for receiving its benefits, not even a belief system. Instead, it is owed to us by virtue of our existence, for this love is the unhindered circuit of our self's reconnection to its source. Its receptivity to us at our most detailed levels of yearning is how life loves each being. In doing so, it simply loves other aspects of itself.

Not even death is the end of love, but the beginning of it in a different form. This is love's beauty; it knows no limits when it is strong enough, and can always generate ever more elements of information about the beloved. That is why following the death of a meaningful person we build memorials, write books, name others after them. As long as there is someone alive who can express information about its object of love, the beloved being will continue to exist.

14

FEELING FEELINGS

It was one of the best feelings I've ever had. [50]

WHATEVER WE WANT, OR do not want, is not the thing for its own sake and in isolation, but because of its anticipated pleasurable effects upon us. According to their means for self-motivation, each being in life participates in this quest towards feeling good. This is a key fact, for when our goal is self-actualization and authenticity, then how we feel is the main compass by which to set our course.

1. Feelings are timeless; there is no such state as a young or an old version of happiness, of love, of sadness, of solitude, etc. Every feeling is equally fresh whenever it appears, regardless of how it occurs.

Feelings cannot age because they are made from our nerves' activations. Just as with live music, they must be activated anew to be experienced.

2. Feelings are our one-dimensional contact with information. The description of what we feel comes from how we think this information will affect us in the short &/or long run. We cannot walk away from our feelings since they inform us about right now. We are nearer to our feelings than to any surface that we can touch with our fingers.

3. Thoughts give our feelings an identity by connecting

them to both specific subject matter and to a storyline in which they eventually find a role. As we interpret their vibratory language, our feelings develop a 2nd dimension through the words and images used to describe them: I feel sad / happy / insecure /hopeful...

To "feel" sad, for example, is to literally *be in contact* with a vibratory landscape and its specific modulation of form, then to identify this topology as the shape of sadness. It's not a coincidence that sad music must have a specific kind of melody and rhythm in order to convey sadness.

4. At any given moment, our contact with life's tonal textures is a background music whose melody implies a distinct kind of scene taking place. Music as an ambient element is ever more popular precisely because people intuitively relate to life's original tonal compositions.

As we interpret their possible significance, our feelings can also give rise to feelings about our feelings. Expanding points of contact then lead to the arrival of ever more feelings, which in some can eventually become overwhelming.

Many people keep their feelings in check out of fear that such a feeling-cascade will carry them away. "Getting carried away" however, is sometimes the best thing that we can do to keep flowing.

"Rationalizing it is incredibly counterintuitive," she said. "It took me a really long time to stop believing that it was real, because it feels so incredibly real." [51]

---

5. Feelings convince us of their vital importance because of an automatic logic that states: a thing must already exist before one can feel (touch) it. Feelings however, are not always as significant as we feel them to be, no matter how strongly. Some of

our feelings may not represent a reality beyond our own neurological readings. These can only be dispelled by our understanding, and not by changes under the control of someone or something else.

Feelings do not necessarily differentiate between a present event and an imagined one. Remember something that once moved you deeply and it will not be long before you are right back into that feeling place; yet it is only in virtual form.

6. Each feeling comes out of a spectrum of all possible feelings. Both circumstances and our self-direction are what catalyze us to feel one way rather than another. We are dependent for the experience of our feelings upon the quality of our nervous system and its education.

Consequently, not everyone can have similar feelings in response to similar inputs. That said, some people are particularly sensitive and so, can feel vibratory energies at their earliest stages of becoming; they have a "sense" about them. We call this having intuitions, premonitions, or hunches.

7. When someone says that they "don't feel" like doing something, they're expressing that, literally, they are not in contact with the same vibratory place as the person who does feel like doing it. To feel good, or to feel bad, expresses in a concrete way the quality of our neurological capacity for experiencing a sensation at that moment.

Feeling good represents that our neurological traffic is active and flowing smoothly while in close contact with current circumstances. At that moment, we literally do feel an inviting neurological flow.

Feeling bad expresses constriction; consequently, we have a reduced capacity to manage and interpret the persistent influx of sensory information moving through our systems. Because we cannot feel our information well enough, we make mistakes of perception, timing, and interpretation.

8. Feelings can take on increasing presence when due to inattention or inaction we ignore or deny them.

9. All of our feelings will register somewhere within us. Depending upon what they are about, they may lay forever dormant, or else burst out.

10. The human repertoire of feelings is universal; what another is feeling is most likely what, to some degree, we have also felt at one time or another. Where people differ is in both the proportions of their feelings, and in the extent to which they are compelled to act them out.

Irritation and full-blown rage, for instance, are made of similar neurological dynamics, only with different amounts of saturation and volume.

...Opened fire in a central street, reportedly in anger that someone had scratched his car.[52]

---

11. At the complete opposite extreme of feelings are numbers. Their word tells us exactly what they do: they numb us from contact with our neurology, and therefore, our capacity to feel.

Whereas feelings can exist without reference to something else, numbers only have value from what they enumerate. This is why businesses can be so completely ruthless with their employees, customers, and especially, competitors. There is rarely a business plan intended to measure feelings, which are something within, whereas what numbers tally is always in evidence.

That notwithstanding, numbers can be a useful form of information and detachment about proportions and progress. Nonetheless, when our lives are centered on them, then their narrow and cool focus leaves us too neurologically contracted to register any feelings about what we are counting. With measurement as our life's chief yardstick, we literally cannot feel. Instead, we keep an eye on whether or not we are "measuring up," no matter what we actually feel in relation to what is being accounted for.

12. We can obtain the best of each universe, that of numbers and that of feelings, when we realize that we are primarily motivated to feel good. Nothing would be worth acquiring if it did not have an emotionally desirable result.

When someone achieves something noteworthy, we do not ask them what they think about it, but rather, how do they feel.

> *For Duran, who has an uncle who is blind, the greatest joy was in seeing a blind person using his creation for the first time. "That was so awesome," he said. "I can't describe the feeling. It was the best."* [53]

Our waking reality is constructed precisely to sensitize us to feel the process of our life's constant becoming. How we *feel* at any given moment is our guide as to where we are going and, if we really want to go there. If not, our feelings also tell us when, and if we are on the right path.

15

IDEAL, YOU DEAL, THEY DEAL

AN IDEAL IS SOMETHING perfect within its own requirements. There is no such thing as an undesirable ideal because desire is the life force that flows through any ideal's veins. The ideal life along human terms would be to obtain whatever we need and want at our command. This isn't asking too much. To be able to transform our reality at will is the only fair dynamic in a life that has the potential for great suffering. Any other arrangement between humans and life has an extremely sadistic component to it.

The ideal is already the ultimate objective of every being; plants and animals intuitively have the integrity not to abandon theirs. No such healthy lifeforms will ever refuse to reach for exactly for what they need and want, and with whatever means they have. Ironically, the one species that can create whatever they envision—human beings—is the one most likely to withdraw from its ideals.

Idealism is nonetheless native to our humanity, and its fulfillment always within our grasp. As humans, we can disassemble and then reassemble raw materials to make this world an increasingly better place in which to live; or a worse one when too many ideals are considered unattainable.

Most of us abandon our ideals because we are culturally discouraged from validating the idea of the ideal itself. In many societies, the adjective "idealistic" is virtually synonymous with "unrealistic" and associated with youth's naiveté. Just the same, humans cannot help but subliminally recognize that the ideal is possible; it is simply that they manage to place it somewhere out of reach, as in heaven. However, if you look at what any heaven consists of, you will see that its parts already exist on earth—just as do those of hell. Heaven is a sensory experience whose terms we all readily grasp: peace, beauty, joy, love, health, prosperity, and so on. We long for a heavenly life even more so because we cannot prevent ourselves from reaching for such ideal states, if only latently within us.

Given that reality is constructed from pure energy guided into virtual form, the ideal is as possible to materialize as is its absence. Ideals are only dismissed as unrealistic because of current global models that actualize the viewpoint of life as a harsh external reality to which we must adapt ourselves to survive. This paradigm forces people to live life at its most oppressive level: survival as a zero-sum game, with enough only for those who grab what they want before someone else does.

The ideal is not a goal that must be abandoned due to life's so-called realities. Instead, the challenges and the obstacles towards it are part of the adventurous playing -field that is life. Any complications along the way are natural participants in the process, and not the proof of our unrealism. In fact, our successes come from a willingness to accept, even to embrace, the changes needed for our ideals to manifest. The more we do so, the easier it is for others to do the same.

Once we realize the community that life represents, then we automatically recognize that the ideal for all is simply an extension of our self-interests. And once you take it for granted that your external circumstances are created from within yourself, then there is no need to scramble for the most advantageous position within a limited pool of resources; no need to let go of your ideals. On the contrary, you can now insist upon them.

16

Conceptual Detergent

It is futile to ask for a problem-free life since obstacles and their solutions are a natural part of learning, growth, adventure, self-actualization, and whatever else at all levels, calls for a response.

Such states as doubt, resistance, disease, apprehension, fear, and so on, *must* feel uncomfortable to force us to pay attention to their vital messages as to where we are and where we might be headed. Otherwise, if unbalanced states felt comfortable then we would never be motivated to remedy them and gradually, surprisingly, we would fall apart.

The art of being as relaxed as possible within discomfort and uneasiness starts with first understanding the temporary nature of our sensations of distress, then to breathe deeply and begin to move through them with a minimum of meanings in mind. This approach optimizes our capacity to be in the moment and, like a cat landing on its feet, to ride out the process of things "righting" themselves.

A solution to any setback develops as soon as we focus away from the solidity of our experience and instead, view it as an energized concept that surfaced out of our deep vibratory landscapes. This softened description immediately triggers the process by which problems dissolve on their own—as they must. Within the information of any problem is also that of its dissolution.

This is to say: get more into the problem, face it, and the spaces between its parts reveal themselves, thus disassembling its solidity into granularity, one which eventually disperses into a solution—a word whose very definition is: elements suspended within a medium and thus, capable of fluidity. In the case of a problem, just as for any of our experiences, we are the medium for its existence *and* for its solution.

The more practiced we become at simply processing the moment without giving it meaning, the more balanced and composed we remain through any difficulties—and the fewer we tend to have. In parallel, we can more easily bear being in suspense while the situation reorients itself. It will do so for the better because to undertake any solution is to expel the problem's shaping energy out of the system and, literally, let it express itself—press itself out of our system.

As it is, the deforming effects of repressed energies are usually the tonal source of most of our life problems. The more we vent these vibrations, the smoother our lives become. Any such expressive process requires us to minimize our fears and their associated feelings; it asks us to avoid getting ahead of ourselves into assumptions and speculations as to what will happen. Instead, we focus our energies into visualizing the point where the difficulty has been solved—but without wondering how it will do so. Trust this process and you will find that you intuitively sense what to do when, and in what way.

Our sincere desire for a solution is already influential in its truth and this acts as a catalyst for the intuitive layers of our being to draw out the problem's solution. From our source substrate—whatever you prefer to call it—life always has the information needed to rearrange elements for our benefit. As a result, at some point along the way a solution will appear on its own. It may nevertheless arrive in a different way and form than the one we would have expected.

Sometimes the repair might feel incomplete, which is more often the case at the beginning of our practices. The missing piece is that either we were not yet willing enough to let go of the situation's problematic components, or we insisted upon a specific outcome whose nature, unbeknown to us, excluded the ultimately desired content. In the course of accumulative experiences, we become better informed and more skilled at how to visualize and phrase what we ask for.

As we progress, the situations can become subtler and in this way, test deeper layers of our concepts about self and life. Not because we must become deserving by being tested, but because the coarser filaments must be twilled away for us to live a life whose fabric is made from a finer weave. In parallel, our fresh demonstrations of skill will only increase our self-confidence. Over time, we will see patterns emerge that illustrate our personal styles and vulnerabilities, and we will come to appreciate how each subsequent difficulty addresses whatever remains in need of strengthening.

The more we cultivate our capacity to feel our customized sensory information, to act upon inner prompts, and to follow our intuitions, the more we become an organic human being, one whose root animal self is fully engaged even during social situations—what I like to call: a humanimal, a rare being in our overly socialized societies. If we are deeply anchored into the commitment to live on such authentic terms, with creativity and self-realization as our priorities, then through a kind of irresistible directional urge, we readily know the right thing to do in most situations—we can "sense" it.

To "sense" what to do is an invaluable ability because it represents that we are plugged into life at its deepest levels. We are now able to receive guidance for not only this moment's solution and subsequent flow, but in ways that also foresee what we will need in the long run.

The companion part to any problem's resolution is also to see it as it appears. "As it appears," means to read the text of the situation for the implied story that it tells about our ideas on reality and self. Unflinching receptivity to the "what is" of a difficulty lets us fully uproot it by illuminating its information with our strongest light. Unless we do this, the next time that this conceptual stressor appears in another venue—possibly more entrenched—we will have to do the same work, and be older in the process.

This dynamic also applies to the problems that we try to spare others from experiencing, which is not always a good idea. Depending upon what the challenge is, each person must solve their own root concepts about life and themselves within it. If they are not allowed to do so, they will eventually have an even bigger difficulty to surmount, one that excludes the assistance of even the most charitable amongst us.

When we feel that our problems arose because somewhere along the line we did not do the right thing, does that mean we got it wrong? No, we got it real.[54] What manifested in the past accurately represented the dominant voices and actors of the circumstances, including those of our own egos. Could we have done it better? Who knows, because what came out was the best that we did; it represents what neurologically happened.

What we could have done is only speculation, a plausible alternative path not taken, whereas what happened was where we went. No need to feel regret though, because life is about learning "to be" better, and the naked quality of our deficient actions can be an inspirational springboard to improve under future circumstances.

The faults of the past usually come from having been carried away by the inertia of a situation rather than by our own self-direction. By default, we did not exercise our options to reflect upon the flow of events so as to let the optimal path speak for itself. Therefore, the circumstances' own egos[55] played themselves out, taking us along with them. Then we wonder, "How did I get here?"

This is not to say that spontaneity and letting go do not have their place, because they do—very much so. The difference comes from realizing the quality and consequences of what is happening while they are part of our moment, as opposed to realizing them only in hindsight. There will always be many opportunities to come under the spell of circumstances or to get into the spirit of events, but that does not remove from us the option to cast our own spells, and to act out of our own spirit. [56]

For any lifestyle that wants to minimize future problems, the root question is: which neurological map is going to rule? [57] Is it that of being stimulated by temporary external prompts—the impulse buys, the triggers to anger, the intimidations to withdraw, the inertia of not wanting to try? Each of these synaptic maps has its own imperatives of action and restraint.

Our best ally in filtering through our choices is the internal compass that navigates us from within. This virtual observer watches our life story unfold, feeling by feeling, thought by thought, action by action, and directs it with enough of a temporal buffer to create the changes that we desire and at a rate we can readily assimilate.

Whatever the nature of our problems, their effects of triggering neurological disorientation in us often causes us to feel as if we have been thrown into the air without a safety net. At such moments, we do not yet understand what to make of our options and therefore, feel that we must be prepared for anything at all. As a result, our fears and weakest self-concepts might well take center stage.

This default to vulnerability is natural; when confronted with demanding challenges, we often overlook our accomplishments and sense only our weaknesses. Consequently, when under pressure, we might slip into the sense of a reality without control, one where we can only hope that complications will somehow resolve themselves. With practice, these default impressions will fall away ever faster from the time of their onset. In part because, from small to large, our successes in connecting deliberate inner activities with external outcomes will embolden us to apply a proof-based faith to ever-larger projects.[58]

Although every degree of discomfort has the potential to arouse us to take remedial action, we are best served by addressing small instances of unease before they assume monolithic proportions and entrench into chronic states. It is a fact that navigating the rapids of any healing process can be a rocky ride; it takes a lot of trust in life. However, the more we rise to the occasion of any difficulties, the more we realize that everything can be transformed for the better, and that every such process is essential to the best that we can achieve.

17

Freedom's Wilderness

Many secretly long to be wild and free but few of us genuinely are. Most of the time we are sandwiched between the expectations of our upbringing, and those of our self-censorship. Even so, within us is the heart of the wild self whom we spend our entire lives trying to actualize. How well we succeed in this goal is largely determined by where we locate our life's playing field: is it within the social sphere, or within the universal one? Depending on where it is, we have different access to the means for fulfilling our wild potential.

Though every culture incorporates an awareness of the universe, a society's priorities are always self-centered and any universal perspective will be relegated to religion and philosophy, when not actively suppressed. Societies do not ask for our whole self, but direct us to fit in—the essence of conformity. They rarely include the needs of a person's inner life, and only address its symptoms when it seems unbalanced and acts out, thereby threatening social constructs.

The fact is that even as they provide for basic infrastructures, all societies are a form of theatre, of fiction, and of play-acting whereby scripts are written and assigned by a society's culture and traditions. For its local character each culture invariably depends upon "sets," and "actors" who behave according to their designated roles in function-related costumes. Moreover, as with all theatrical productions, the actors and the props reference a more engaging reality that continues unrelentingly off-stage and is located at increasing and deepening levels of universality.

"I don't wear the right kind of pants to run this company," ... He was barefoot as he spoke, and wearing blue jeans.
Steve Jobs after Apple's Board of Directors downgraded him in the mid 1980s.[59]

Our social framework offers material templates, but often at the cost of one's self-actualization. If we do not choose our own playing field, the social one will be the default setting. However, if we want to completely actualize then we will need to live within a universal paradigm. Unlike the social playing field, the universal field is the only one of the two that contains information about both our inner and our outer lives. It has complete knowledge about every being and directs each along life's basic thrust, which is to live as freely and as creatively as possible.

If the universal world disappeared, then so would all societies. However, if societies disappeared, the universe would not; on the contrary, it would thrive. No matter how extreme the environment, nature has its own ways of surviving into ever-newer forms. This invincible spirit for creative adaptation also courses through us when we live within the universal framework; from it we are constantly guided to intuitively navigate our way through any society and its changes.

The ideal balance is, of course, to be able to use both social and universal frames of reference, but with priority being given to the latter. In this way, we continue to live within the social one in its accurate place as a subset of the universal. Such a prioritization leaves us free to act according to our truest nature, and independently of any society's self-serving validations. Furthermore, we become more effective in our own society since, as part of their wholeness, universal forces must contain all information about social ones.

When we orient ourselves within a universal frame of reference we inevitably keep our neurology engaged in its most fundamental way; we act out of the same sensory dimensions as those experienced by genuinely wild beings. Their vitality receives intuitive prompts from a much deeper pool of instructions than can ever be accessed by a socially dominated neurology. The capacity of animals to be guided towards their needs is equally accessible to humans because an underlying guidance comes to each from the exact same source.

Whether it is tapped into or not, this natural connection is available during our entire lifetime, and it is never too late to reach for it. There is no difference in an animal's instinct for finding food and a person's need to feed their individual and professional goals, whatever they may be: from nutrition, to a rich wardrobe, to a purpose in life, to entertainment, to health. What differs between beings is the repertoire of realities that each creature gets to perceive and to manipulate through their physicality. Animals usually have no choice but to be free and wild, whereas humans are rarely either.

What is freedom? We know that we cannot look to a social medium for a complete answer. By its very nature as a matrix for group collaboration, a society seeks control over multiple aspects of the individuals that comprise it. Even in more liberal societies, freedom, especially the expressive kind, is highlighted as being risky—ironically enough, not for the group but for the individual. The Western world provides many examples of artists whose wild exercises of creative freedom are mentioned in the same breath as their mental imbalances—true or not.

Freedom means being the only one who decides when and how you are going to navigate yourself. Freedom is to feel as we do, and to have the space to explore those feelings, regardless of where they lead. To be free to think as we wish without having to compare it to what we ought to be thinking. It is to willingly assess our perceptions as deeply as possible, and regardless of their implications. Our personal freedom is the medium within which we actualize into physicality the life potential at the core of our hearts. Paradoxically, the most sophisticated and free form of wilderness is to be wild as a socialized person.

Contrary to its image of mindless pursuit, someone with true freedom protects themselves through their exercise of self-imposed limits. Without them, they would eventually go too far and meet even more constricting public forces than those of their own private boundaries. As with musical strings, limits create desirable and necessary tensions. We need rules for any game to feel the thrill of ourselves playing it on its terms, and to have specificity of action and of thought. Moreover, just as water finds its own containment, freedom eventually finds its own levels of stability according to context, even as it seeks to maintain its flow.

Our outer freedom starts with assuming responsibility for the direction of our inner one. Within this world is where we can illuminate our motivations, and to far more subtle degrees than those found in any judicial system. Here in our inner world, there is great freedom of being. It is all the greater because only its possessor can discern its true contents. It is a secure place to which no one else has a right. In it, we can afford to be bold in both our dreams and in our self-honesty for here we are truly alone and need answer to no one, except in those circumstances where our conscience calls for it.

Within us is where we have the possibility to fine-tune our conceptual and emotional behaviours, precisely because only we witness this freedom. This access is not just one of our human options, but increasingly necessary in order to be guided through rapid global changes of roles, traditions, and values. To live with increasing detail, to refine ourselves from the inside out, is to live a life of luxury in that word's root sense of "light" (lux). From there, we process ever-more exquisite sensory information; we hear ever finer existential music. That we care to participate in our own transcendence transforms us for the better and improves the whole world along with us.

Meanwhile, contemporary anarchic behaviour is accepted only from those with glamorous roles as artists, celebrities, politicians, or persons of great wealth. The rest of the time, freedom is given a fierce and wild face, one associated with unpredictable dynamics, if not danger. By way of reinforcing this socially anxious relationship with wilderness, we generally pretend that our bodies do not function like those of other animals, bodily fluids and all. We also routinely dress in ways that are an unspoken condemnation against being fully in contact with life's textures, against being naked.

Not least, wilderness is presumed to exercise senseless violence and, therefore, is to be shunned. This more accurately describes impoverished and marginalized urban areas than it does any wilderness, where every form of being implicitly follows specific guidelines for behaviours and interactions.

Of all living systems that use freedom responsibly, those of every wilderness rank among the highest, and those of human societies among the very lowest. Once we appreciate the beautiful orchestration of wilderness' interacting forces, then we will long to possess such a choreography in ourselves. Deep down, we recognize it as our existential home base.

Just as wild animals and other untamed creatures do, we also have access to a trustworthy internal positioning system. The thrust of its influence is always our state of wholeness and its attainment of needed resources–including in the case of humans, socially constructed ones. The more we align ourselves with this wild inner flow, the more we courageously venture out into all unknowns, including social ones.

Direct contact with the fully activated present moment is the freest and most vitalizing relationship that life can offer us, and living spontaneously is the inevitable by-product of claiming our freedom to thus travel through life. By being engaged in our Now we flow along shores that reveal unprecedented scenery, as well as newly discovered opportunities for self-expansion.

Because our thoughts have specificity to them, conceptual freedom is one of the richest ones to exercise. If you can be free to genuinely think information through for yourself, then you will find an optimal and intuitive way into beneficial actions and insights. The universal framework guarantees it, for even the most artificially civilized person is not excluded from life's self-organizing processes.

When we let this dynamic have its way with us then with the perspective of time, we readily understand how we came to be where we are, and in the way that we went–regardless of how much our behaviour appears unfathomable when taken in isolation. Even the disorderly events that emerged from our quest for authenticity become part of an ongoing orderly dynamic. Nor are changes of destination proof of confusion; any authentic way will inevitably require acting out and modifying various aspects of oneself.

Our self is not a single "I," but a series of bundled channels seeking to align into an interflowing way of being. Our social self is simply the external cylinder, the visible cable that keeps all the hidden ones in parallel. In collaboration, our deepest being is the constant reconciler of all the threads that weave us into existence.

The information that we trust and act upon is what determines the paths we must follow. The one leading to self-actualization is always within reach so long as we're sincerely ready to accept the changes needed to get there. We need not fear to go with them because our imaginations, our brains, and our bodies are constructed so that they will increase their capacities and skills correspondingly. The universe itself will assist; it has to, for it is each of us.

I could have been a contender. I could have been somebody—instead of a bum, which is what I am.
Marlon Brando, On the Waterfront, 1954

At every moment, we have immense power to invent ourselves; for the most part, each human being has as much the potential to be a leader as to be a beggar in the street; each can also become the other. In just the same way that a tree draws water to its peak, so a thirst for our deepest goals also draws life. All it takes is for each of us to tap into our native courage to live as an organic being; our objectives then create their own directions and materials.

Unlike humans, wild creatures never ask for permission to fullfill themselves. Without hesitation, without apology, and to the full capacity of their reach, they seek what they want from their environments. Most people, meanwhile, are either justifying or pleading for their preferences. We cultivate conceptual restrictions that cause us to put tests and filters on the things that we naturally want, filters that exclude our authenticity, even as we long for it. We also deny others the right to live their own self-realized existence—perhaps out of anxiety that they might be right about their liberation, and we wrong in our enclosures.

In complete contrast, animals and plants make the most of every resource available to them. This naive and forthright state of "going for it" was the one from which our own being arose. The metaphor of the tree in the Garden of Eden tells us that to leave an automated and guided existence—to which all other creatures still subscribe—is to take on conscious responsibility for every detail of our lives. The benefits gained from eating this fruit of knowledge are far greater than their price, for its nutrition catalyzes a way back to this same wild existence; except that this time, it can include social goals. Not just for basic sustenance, but for the freedom and joy to create for its own sake.

In order to maximize our sense of being alive we need to cultivate both universal wildness and social skills. Their collaboration creates a landscape filled with opportunities and beauties that are beyond the ability of what any society alone can offer, and beyond the limits of any unsocialized wilderness.

The self-organizing principles of the external wilderness apply equally to an organic society, which can only appear when all within it are truly free. Even though many societies claim to embody such a system, they have no other vision but to promote bureaucracies that reduce people to numbers and sociological theories.

Most social institutions practice a connecting-the-dots technique of moving from one point to another. They use the straight lines of rules that are based upon the averaging of templated human beings. Straight lines do not foster authenticity but require and empower rulers. The curved line predominates within us, for we ultimately live by feelings.

If we want to achieve both freedom and self-realization, then we need to question the information that directs us into action. The more clearly we understand our key words, the more our thoughts can serve our goals. Instead of dominating us, the words that we both send and receive will then help us synchronize our universal and social experiences of life.

When we accept responsibility for the information that we receive from our unhindered perceptions, then we have the daring to become our truest self without the need for anyone's authorization or validation. We will still want to govern ourselves in cooperation with others, but only to the extent that anyone has a right to expect it.

Without guilt, we will sense the natural limits for how much we must give of ourselves, how much we need to keep, and how much we can take from another. If people affirmed the ideal of each one being their truest selves, then a thriving organic society would emerge without the need for any artificial incentives or controls. The hallmark of a truly civilized being or society is that they want to protect the dignity of others as well as their own. To do so, lets people be their full selves, each according to their nature.

Democracy means that each one of us is responsible for the government that we have. In parallel, the government is itself responsible for facilitating its citizens' activism for an ever-better society. By its very nature, the democratic model recognizes the high value of each person, even when it inadequately implements the educational investment that this political relationship *must* make.

Without providing access to the education needed for nuanced and sophisticated forms of thinking, a democratic society cultivates its decay from within. Pure survival or greed as the primary engines thus maintain their merciless supremacy, regardless of technological or cultural sophistication. Within such a game, situations and players may change forms and positions, but as each being looks out for itself at major costs to others, the battles of supremacy then continue.

However, when we see reality as manifesting vibratory landscapes that rise and fall according to acts of imagination and ideals, then we can dispense with competition and instead, cooperate to create a world whose resources benefit everyone. Individuality and prosperity cannot help but then flourish. This global teamwork is not an effort to homogenize the human experience, but rather to minimize–through pooled information and a collective vision–the time spent acquiring the resources common to all of us for our basic survival.

We human beings can create heaven on earth. It starts by taking responsibility for our own life's fulfillment. This is pragmatic rather than selfish for, as the Sufi story goes, only the person with an overflowing bowl has enough to share with others.

18

Is It 4 Real ?

I took my time & when I saw the ring, asked "Is it real?" [60]

Reality is not a stand-alone element that surrounds us like air or water. Instead, reality is first an internal event, one assembled by our nervous system's activities as processed by our brains. Because reality starts within, disagreements as to what is real or unreal readily arise. To resolve the reality of something, be it a feeling, a perception, a thought, or a dream, we first need to ask the question: "in what form does this reality exist?"

The answer tells us how many dimensions any given reality has. Its dimensionality then tells us if this reality must be limited to an individual (as with a dream, a hallucination, a certain feeling,) or if it is accessible to the world at large (as with a mountain, rain, an idea expressed in words.)

Because feelings have one dimension of physicality, they can only be experienced individually, even when expressed to another. As such, there is no point in denying the actuality of anyone's feelings; what to do about them must first follow their reality's acknowledgment...as a feeling.

Ideas have at least two dimensions since they can be shared with others through texts and images, which are also made of two dimensions. All ideas are real; however, their fulfillment into more concrete realities requires that further dimensions be added.

Objects in external space have three dimensions plus a fourth involving change, and framed as time. Any such objects' reality should be accessible to all in its area.

The ease with which we can agree on these 4-Dimensional kinds of realities has a trap though, one that hypnotizes us into viewing majority opinion as the first test of any reality's authenticity. This premise, is however, not valid since what is externally perceived is quickly qualified by verbal descriptions that are based on each perceiver's experiences and backgrounds. Consequently, to try to convince someone that their version of reality is false inevitably triggers their resistance, since it asks them to deny their experience of the very nervous system needed for their agreement with us. Delusional persons are genuinely frightened because they're convinced that their perceptions are accurate.

Actuality, Not Reality –Slogan for TruTV

Reality is best defined as whatever existence we feel compelled to deal with, regardless of whether anyone else agrees that it is real. In support of this definition, there are many examples of people who are convinced of their reality in ways that to most seem obviously wrong.

Somewhere in the world, right now, there are people who believe that they should not have their arms or legs.[61] They go to surgeons to have them removed so that they might feel "whole." Others think aliens have replaced their relatives.[62] Some are convinced that they are missing organs, or are actually dead.[63] There are also people who cannot feel pain, while others cannot recognize faces. [64]

That the vast majority of people can feel pain and do recognize familiar faces does not change the fact that normality is a variation on the theme of neurological relationships, just as abnormality is.

The poignant examples here are extreme, but what about cultural concepts that deny human potential? How does anyone of us know whether or not we have been fully informed on what is humanly possible? For the full answer, we each must investigate life for ourselves and be open to whatever we discover, regardless of mainstream assertions or denials—many of which the filters of time have discredited.

The brevity of our life span gives the impression of perceptual constancy, but a stroll through history reveals a variety of worldviews—many hard to understand as ever having been accepted. A travelogue assembled by Medieval European explorers documented, with eyewitness drawings, the foreign natives that they encountered. However, these illustrations show people with one large ear on their stomachs, or else giants 9 to 12 feet tall, said to be found in Patagonia by Magellan and his crew in 1520.[65]

In his first century encyclopedia, *Naturalis Historia*, Pliny the Elder relates voyagers' descriptions of Hindu people with only one leg and foot. They were known as *Monopods*, or as *Skiapods* because they lay on their backs when it was very hot and shaded themselves with their upheld leg and foot.[66]

Regardless of the improbability of an encounter with such peoples today, strange creatures are constantly being found, thanks to ever more probing technologies. Meanwhile, via theories of multiple universes, physicists are increasingly telling us that reality is neither as it appears to be, nor constant. Enough so for us to wonder: what is reality all about? The question and answer both, always reduce to what is "my" reality about, for it is the only one we ever get to live.

Ultimately, your own experience is the main determinant for what is real for you. How successfully we each convince others of a given reality is a secondary matter to what we actually believe to be real, enough so for us to become anxious if we ignore it. The fact is that we cannot escape from the impressions of reality created by our nervous systems. Only by accepting new information can we change how our nerves' synapses fire and so, potentially transform our perceptions of reality.

Debates on what is real are misguided in their efforts to obtain universal agreement on everything. Such unanimity requires the impossible: identical nervous systems, cultures, and experiences.

When we insist that only what is real for everyone is truly real, then we miss out on life's main activity: variations on themes, including the theme of being human. Witness that there exist 400,000–1,000,000 species of beetles, 28,000+ varieties of potatoes, 3,000+ of rhododendrons, so, how many variations of humans? Unique ways of being are vital to the evolution of life's creative potential; even more so, given the fact that only an individual's inner life and not groupthink, can spark the creation of ideas and ideals.

Our finest global scenario is to share the same realities on life's vital resources and then to let go of the losing battle that seeks to direct people's inner realms. After all, we cannot so far disprove that those who hear inner voices, or who see ghosts, are not simply tapping into other fields of being.

In the late 1980s, enough people heard disembodied voices to establish a movement. Those with "voice hearing," their friends as well as health care professionals, are still lobbying for this to be framed as a healthy state. Three thousand years ago, they would not have had to, because hearing voices from within was not then an illness, but a respected ability.[67]

Nevertheless, the idea of agreeing upon one reality is still widely used as an index for our sanity, precisely because reality is presented as hard and inflexible. Thus, we are not supposed to accept different neurological firings on the theme of reality's variations. Though reality does have certain "rules of the game" that make it seem as if we have few options to shape it, just the opposite is true. Reality is highly malleable; its inherent suppleness offers the same freeform potential as any art medium.

There is a growing sense that the properties of the universe are best described not by the laws that govern matter but by the laws that govern information.[68]

Just as colours take on shape when applied, and stem cells differentiate into tissues when catalyzed, so our life changes through the information that we let influence us. For better or worse, this means "anything goes." Life will bring into being whatever has the necessary materials to be itself, and for however long it can last.

There is a misimpression that "creating reality" means you should be able to pop realities out of thin air. Possible in principle, but upon closer inspection you'll notice that any new creation is always a transformation of something else. Even objects arriving out of nowhere have changed oxygenated space. Further, thinking in terms of "transforming" our reality makes it more natural to imagine that we can do so. But whether creating or transforming, we first need to manage the contents of our own imagination.

All imagination is simply a way of changing relationships of information; it is the process of giving something further sensory aspects without yet being faced with it. To the degree of its commitment, our imagination's vibratory activity directs the transmutation of energy from virtuality into actuality. You simply need to suspend your disbelief long enough to let this new way of thinking offer proof of its effectiveness, which it will. In time, you come to see that the limits by which you live are created by your own ideas far more than by what is actually possible.

Instead of a 2-Dimensional surface upon which we can paint, reality is made of conceptual and emotional energy patterns whose material forms we "draw" out according to what we feel we deserve, and according to what we think life will allow. By living within the paradigm of reality as an art form, we catalyze the outer world's capacity to morph into directions in which we want it to go.

Morphing is the transformation of one thing into another in a self-adjusting way, as with marbleized paper. This organic process spontaneously creates a believable impression of before and after as part of a reasonable relationship—sufficiently so to make something feel real. The impression of a plausible reality is all we need since we are not in the habit of dissecting each moment to test whether or not it is actually there. If it feels real, it *is* real for as long as that feeling exists.

One of the sleights of hand in the play of life is that when we like the reality that we live by, we do not question too far why or how it came to be because we're too eager to enjoy it. Even if we did need a clear explanation for how a lucky change manifested in time, we would find that it involved previously unknown information that can be retrofit as a missing link such that the new circumstances make sense and seem durable.

Reality's raw limits must feel and appear logically secure for the sake of both time-forward planning as well as for our sanity. The extent to which real seems to be "really real" is a necessary requirement for life's tones to have sufficient tension between its spectrum of "yes" and "no." Nevertheless, any transformations and their related explanations are steps out of our usual horizontal linearity and arise out of energy vertically directed into specific forms through information. The dynamics between horizontal and vertical is precisely why I describe our source field of concepts as a "crossfield".

Any emphasis on outer measurements as a test of reality is limited, given that our inner reflections reveal facts in ways that are otherwise not in evidence. A full life inextricably contains both realms. That said, the inner world's equal status with the outer world's remains undone. This is understandable, for such an equivalence absolutely correlates with the equal valuation of both male *and* female energies–yang and yin.

Consequently, current scientific proofs continue to rely solely upon concrete objects of study. The efficiency of this approach is that when a dozen scientists have validated any such externalized experiment, then there is no need for hundreds more to do so. However, some phenomena can only be appraised internally—their reality proven by frequency and not by outer examinations.

If you repeatedly have experiences of synchronicity, precognition or telepathy, then their frequency is what persuades you of their reality, and not the fact that you can activate them on demand. Thus, it might take reports of hundreds of thousands of such private individual experiences before conventional scientists validate a sixth, seventh, or further sense.[69]

Nonetheless, when you understand the probabilistic nature of the quantum world as the shaper of the actual atomic one, then you can readily accept that extra-sensory realities are not only possible, but inevitable. In the end, what matters most to each of us is the reality that we undergo, however unconventional and mysterious.

The "true" reality is whatever anyone feels to be real, for however long they are in that perceptual state. It may be a reality with a minority of one, but its effect is as true for that individual as if the majority had adopted it.

19

NOTHING REALLY MATTERS

The nature of a quantum entity is "conceptual," i.e. it interacts with... an entity made of ordinary matter... in an analogous way as a concept interacts with a human mind.[70]

THE IDEA THAT REALITY CAN be transformed at will is only 1° of separation from the known workings of quantum mechanics. Quantum behaviours force physicists to speak as if they were both scientists and mystics.

Since the goal of physics is to tell us how our shared reality is constructed, only a few established facts are needed to confidently state that concepts are the seeds for all physical materializations. The value of referring to a scientific foundation is simply that it lets us practice conceptual techniques without requiring us to also adopt a belief system.

We will not only be relying on scientific facts, however, because constant proofs are essential for us to develop a rock-solid faith. Deep faith based upon proof is imagination's best friend for undertaking bold visualizations with a minimum of resistance and hesitation.[71]

Atoms in Apples

4D physicality is very simple at the atomic level; there, 3 distinct particles build up everything we experience and everything we experience with. The three are: protons, electrons, and neutrons, each with their respective charge: positive, negative, and neutral. The relationships of these particles with one another construct all things in the macro world, including us. For example: in chemistry, "O" stands for oxygen, and "H" is for hydrogen. The bonding of two atoms of hydrogen to one of oxygen creates a molecule of water—H_2O.

Where before each element's form was an ungraspable gas, an invisible substance through which we would always fall, now bonded, we have a tangible and visible liquid that we can drink, swim in, or wash with. This formula's reliability exists across the known universe. And yet, we must go beyond the atomic world to find out what atoms are made of. For this adventure we enter the quantum realm.

If an atom were scaled up so that its nucleus was the size of the Earth, the distance to its closest electrons would be 2.5 times the distance between the Earth and the sun. In between is nothing at all. If so much of reality is built on emptiness, then what gives rocks and other objects their form and bulk? [72]

"Quantum" is a mainstream word, as in the expression "quantum leap." Size is not what quantum is about but rather, absolute transition from one state to another. A quantum jump is where you go from, say, 1 to 2 without any possible in-between states such as 1½, 1¾, or any other fraction. Only one-shot levels can be attained.

Before quantum mechanics were noticed, physicists presumed that the same set of laws applied to everything. But as it turns out, the quantum world is free from several important rules of atomic realities and instead, offers multiple-choice and contradictory states of being. Because of quantum mechanics' unique properties, physicists now differentiate between two realms of physicality: quantum and classical. Whereas classical physics say that something is either on or off, quantum mechanics have no such absolutes and allow for yes and no to co-exist simultaneously—sometimes with a "maybe" thrown in; this is known as "superposition".

In 2010, scientists at UC, Santa Barbara, demonstrated that a visible object could be moving and not moving at the same time. A quantum particle ("qubit") had transferred its dual state to a metal strip and caused it to both oscillate and to stay still at the very same time. This team of scientists thinks that within two decades we will be able to view an object as large as a child's swing in a state of superposition.[73]

"Entanglement" is another quantum property whereby a pair of particles has a linked existence by way of a shared quantum property, regardless of how far they are separated. If a particle from this pair is physically distanced from the other, and the remaining one has a quantum property changed, such as its spin, this action then instantaneously alters the spin of the particle located many miles away, to the Moon and beyond.

To use an analogy: if you are in an entangled state with someone and you decide to turn your sweater inside out, then the "entangled" sweater that the other person is wearing in another town will simultaneously flip from one side to the other. This effect occurs even if each of you are on different planet.

Thanks to such quantum properties, entire global networks of quantum computers could exist without a single connecting cable between them.

Quantum computers could produce an answer in days or maybe even seconds, whereas the fastest conventional computer would take longer than 13.7 billion years.[74]

When the physicist Daniel Salart and his team separated the particles by only 18 km, the speed at which their entangled simultaneity had to happen was calculated at 10,000 times the speed of light. In classical physics however, light's speed is the sacred upper limit for all matter in motion.[75]

In 2011, the Nobel-winning scientist Luc Montagnier announced that the DNA he had placed in a test tube transferred its code to pure water in other test tubes without direct physical contact between them. Given these conditions, the transfer must have taken place through some kind of transcendental connection. The imprinted code in the completely untouched water then formed enzymes that matched the DNA sequence in the "mother" tube. The result, scoffed at by some scientists, has been called "quantum teleportation of DNA." [76]

Effects at a distance that we can observe are not completely new. Pure potential as a basic physical property was first proposed through tests in 1959. By way of a physical barrier, the field of a magnet was blocked from a particle in its area of influence. Thanks to this blocking, the magnetic field was *incapable* of crossing the solid obstruction; nonetheless, the particle reacted as if it were experiencing the effects of magnetism.[77]

Such experiments showed that the magnetic *potential* alone is enough to cause a particle to react, even when the magnetic and electrical fields are both at zero. Because of the above results, and others, physicists increasingly see the classical Newtonian laws of physicality—once considered rock-bottom—as emerging from a deeper reality, one that follows different rules.[78]

To reconcile quantum reality's seemingly contradictory dynamics, physicists have theorized the existence of the multiverse. According to this hypothesis, the objects and situations of our reality are not events with a single and inevitable, outcome.[79] Instead, each potential reality appears out of an infinite number of possibilities, all of which occur in their own universe, with a fresh one for all variables at play. In one universe, you're reading this material, in another, you're not, and in yet another, this book wasn't written.

To use an everyday example, this would represent that everyone can win a lottery. Since all sets of numbers have a chance at being selected somewhere, it is no longer a question of picking the winning numbers; instead, the skill would be in finding a vibratory way to occupy the universe where your chosen numbers are selected.[80]

As it is, the field of physics has for some time included theories of universes with holographic natures such that each piece of the universe contains information about itself as a whole.[81] Further, a recent theory describes the possibility of something coming out of nothing—particles being extracted from a vacuum.[82] With only a little stretch, this sounds like imagination's capacity for transforming materiality.

The ultra-small scales theorized upon below even the quantum world explain part of our ability to access potential being in a purely conceptual way. Infinitesimal size is especially striking in string theories. "Strings" are hypothetical sub-quantum particles of 10^{-33} cm: that is, one-millionth of a billionth, of a billionth, of a billionth, of a centimeter.[83] All quantum properties would thus arise from the various vibrations of these one-dimensional strings.

According to the above kinds of worldviews, it is plausible

to consider that reality is simply what exists under a given set of circumstances. Change them—for example, by your thoughts on a subject—and you occupy a different reality. This kind of arrangement is essentially a form of simplicity and economy.

When you add up all of the variables that could exist, across all beings and spaces, plus how much energy it would take for each of their combinations to be experienced, then it only makes practical sense that any reality should be virtual and conceptual instead of fundamentally solid.

20

Now is a Stem Cell

"Now what?!"

Now's quiet secret is that it doesn't exist. What we call "now" is an ongoing nano-flash of change that creates the vivid impression of a present moment—nevertheless, it is merely an impression.

The hard presence of any Now is ungraspable; it disappears as it starts. Now never stays; it cannot. We are always entering and exiting a new now, one whose reality is constructed from past information that briefly sparkled into embodiment, only to become memory.

Now seems to offer motion, but it offers a still image of what was. We think that a given situation lasts over time, in minutes, hours, years, but only thanks to the way in which we carry over the contents of each "now" from its previous view, just as the current photo of a flip book sets up the next one to create the illusion of actual streaming movement.

We can move our texts and images forward, but we can never completely pin down the 4-Dimensional nows that they represent—these are far more defined by their absence than by their presence. We take photographs specifically because we cannot stop the transformation of each instant's contents into that of the next.

This play of light & sound is our proof of consciousness because to be conscious is to be present with what we know—for now. Our impression of ongoing being is the result of this illusory device: seemingly stable information as to what is, changing to what will be, disappearing into what was. As we continue entering an equally elusive future, we're the ones who stabilize now's evanescence by accepting its constant disappearance. Because now never stands still, is why we can transform our reality by changing the interpretation of the information that we focus upon, moment to moment.

The "Now," sometimes called "the point of power," [84] is precisely that because it is the only life instant when everything going on is in full dimensional alignment: from its 4D physicality, to its origins as a zero-dimensional conceptual state. Because information is thus at its peak state of presence, Now is where life's raw energy is most able to convert what "is" into what "becomes."

To access that transformative potential, we need to reduce now and its "what is" to its simplest form: vibrations. The landscapes that they construct are the surfaces that we make contact with when we say we "feel," and the movements in our feelings are our indications of where we are traveling.

The essence of whatever we feel at any moment embodies a tone, one that joins previous tones and becomes yet another element of an overall vibratory topology. Any now's texture-tone determines if we can be at ease with what is going on, or if we will yearn for something else. When a pleasurable or reassuring "tone" is not felt, its absence then becomes the drawing force that acts in reach of it.

This tone of aching for something has a conceptual blueprint for what 4-Dimensionality could, and should materialize for us to achieve a feeling of satisfaction and wellbeing. This dynamic of expectation is the same one found in relation to hearing a melodious piece of music. As the musical score unfolds into a vibratory panorama, each awaited note has its dedicated place within the ribbon of the entire composition—so it is with our reality.

Creatures of all kinds draw out their needed and wanted realities by using concrete intuitive resonances that are based on direct sensory contact. According to the comfort or discomfort that results from these experiences, so will a creature long for either the same circumstances or, for something better.

A being's tonal reaches can also have the effect of creating something new through both mutations and epigenetics. Epigenetic changes—whereby circumstances cause a DNA's genes to either turn on or off—are brought about by a being's tonal longing to, literally, "feel better" and to be in contact with a more harmonious transition from one sensory experience to the next. When they become genetically entrenched, these changes can be passed on to future generations.

Evolutionists call it "survival of the fittest" as if a change came about only due to external conditions. However, these were the co-authors of a new genetic text rather than the sole source for its collaborator's developing story. Any being's adaptation to environments and to events is simply the natural "drawing out" of a solution in response to its own emotional needs and biological appetites.

This pulse to reach for one's desires animates every creature's being, even though life is itself neutral as to the particulars of each thirst, just as what is painted on a canvas makes no difference to the brushes and to the colours. Only the degree of passion for its appearance determines if a reality (or a painting) eventually comes into being, now, later, or never.

21

Tuning In

If we want to develop our transformative abilities, then we need to think of our life not as filled with solid objects, but with information-shaped energy. This energy is modulated into being by the information that we accept as real, and therefore true.[85] What we think is true also builds our nervous system, whose branches become the roads that we travel with our emotions, perceptions, and concepts of self and reality's possibilities.

According to what concepts are activated, our imagination's vibrations have a specific rhythm and melody to them. Their preverbal modulations arrange themselves into a tonal composition, one that begins the process of adding dimensionality to concepts. The feel of these vibratory textures follows the textual content of both what is desired and, subliminally of what is shunned.

In every instant of our now, we all long for specific tones to either be added or removed from the melody composed by our actions and reactions. These desires, whether unconscious or overt, evoke words and images in us that have the potential to draw out what they represent into full materiality.

Not just our preferences, but what we fear also takes on life when we let it have its way in our imagination. To dwell on our fears only adds more details to what we do not want, and so subtly cultivates its arrival. The cost of reassuring ourselves away from these imagined anxieties is a very taxing way of confirming our needs and wants.

It is far better to practice minimizing our fears and instead to focus on nurturing our ideals. These will be directed by our heart's longings, in combination with our biology's need for ongoing health at all levels, from the transcendental to the physical. The facilitator of this welcome navigation is our own surrender to what comes through from the crossfield of being in the form of guiding information and synchronous meetings.

When it arrives, this imagined-into-being actuality will not obviously violate any of reality's ruling principles so as to appear truly impossible. This is one of the beauties inherent in the concept of "real" reality. Instead of something nonsensical happening, there is the new information that now in its revelation, changes everything in our favor. It comes in a multitude of forms, from an unexpected circumstance, to the arrival of opportunities, to the remembrance of a forgotten detail, to simply fresh information out of the blue. These factors will morph a situation in such a way that it all continues to make sense.

Even when we think in terms of a concept-based reality, we continue to experience our life *as if* it were independent of us and resistant to will. Without these elements, there could be no edges or tensions to define what we experience, nor any weight felt so as to make things matter such that our pleasures and pains are in the balance.

The drawback to this edgy device however, is that if we identify too much with reality's terms of solid being, then we feel convincingly locked into our situations. The question is then whether we have the strength to break through, or else feel deserving enough to be set free. The effect of this immersion into density is that we have to negotiate with external forces on their own restrictive conditions, rather than from our self-actualizing creativity. We then work on the external appearance of things rather than reviewing inwardly the conceptual edifices that are holding this manifestation together.

Instead of doing the heavy lifting by working primarily from the outside in, the most efficient (and interesting) way to achieve any goal is to work from the inside out. From that standpoint, we can draw out the desired changes through our imagination, feelings, and our basic emotional resonances—namely, what is contained in our heart, ideally acting in partnership with our mind.

The "feel" for any imagined reality starts with these emotionally pulsed vibratory textures. Before becoming defined imagery and language, these vibes gather into a kind of orchestrated existential "music," the most fitting word for information emerging as being. In a direct way, the music to which we respond to is a one-dimensional restatement of our own deep story; the quantum field's fluctuations have thus gone full circle and returned us to our native landscapes.

22

IN THE SPIRIT OF THINGS

"It's probably, if not definitely unconstitutional, and it's incredibly mean-spirited," she said. [86]

ANY HUMAN SPIRIT IS THE lightest form of feelings and intentions that arise from our individual ways of being and influence us into action. To be "spiritual" is to acknowledge this influence and to interact with it. Contrary to its public image, being spiritual does not automatically equate to being "good"; spirituality can go either way. A spirit is no different in nature than any other finely grained material.

No spiritual state guarantees solely by its spirituality that goodwill motivates it, or that it must lead to beneficial outcomes. This would be equal to saying that all odors are pleasant by virtue of being constructed from very small particles.

There is no way of ascribing a favourable or an unfavourable value to a spiritual motive until we have looked at its effects upon ourselves and upon the rest of the world. Unfortunately, since to speak about spirituality is usually seen as proof of one's goodwill, hearing someone do so often deflects taking a closer look at the speaker's own behaviour and character.

The fact is that people in the pursuit of a spiritual life vary in kindness and in cunning. While many who call themselves spiritual are sincere people who want purpose and community in their life, a spiritual quest alone says nothing about a spiritual seeker's deeper motives. Within their spiritual realm, each person continues to be a totality of how they are and of what they do. People use the word "spirit" in their own way and for their own purposes, including for exploiting others. You cannot know anyone's actual spiritual personality until you know how they behave under a variety of pressures.

"They just keep pulling things out of their playbook," he said. (Steve Gill on 'brand-name industry's evolving efforts to prevent generic competition in pharmaceuticals'.) [87]

Spirit's equal opportunity paths toward what is either beneficial or harmful—and all degrees in between—doesn't imply that life encourages harm, but neither does it discourage it. Only a human being's creative free-will permits all to find out for themselves the character and limits of their creations, each of which starts with a specific spiritual orientation.

Regardless of the intended materiality, what makes spirituality worth cultivating is its practice of fine-tuning our feelings, thoughts, and actions. By cultivating our spiritual seeds, a far more solid foundation exists under whatever kind of an outcome is desired. A genuinely spiritual person deliberates upon and nurtures their seed motivations; they intuitively recognize the spiritual domain's supportive role in their goals' successful materializations.

Such spiritual awareness is available to all who reach for it. Those people whose intentions are to take advantage of others also spend time contemplating; they too have a spiritual life that helps them to succeed in their objectives, just as the well-intentioned do. Most of us have heard the term "mean-spirited" or "in the spirit of exploitation," and we understand those characterizations to describe the distasteful core of their hosts.

If we want to know the spiritual basis for our own motivations, we need to develop an ongoing presence in our inner world from where we can see our spirit's true character. It cannot help but appear, since any spirit eventually expresses itself as specific drives, thoughts, feelings and ultimately, deeds.

As a rule, reviewing our spiritual states is a form of basic maintenance. Unless we regularly look at the intentions that pilot our spirit, it is all too easy for the spiritual level to promote and lobby for its dominant content. Gradually, it can then increase the dimensionality of its unedited expressions. We call that "coming under the influence," "seduction," or any other way that expresses taking on a passive role in what we are led to do, or to be.

That is why people who have turned off their executive functioning, say through unconditional trust or through intoxicants, can do foolish and dangerous things. Due to their lack of self-observation, no one was at home to filter a spiritual orientation's increasing momentum and thus, see where it was leading—taking its host along in the process.

Spiritual Matters

All-out spiritual engagement is the destination of an authentic physical life—each in combination with the other, and to the exclusion of neither. Spirit and matter are opposite ends on the same continuum, and the translation of a spiritual impulse into its physicality is unavoidable because every energy-seed always seeks to organize more materiality unto itself. If you look at any offer, be it spiritual salvation or detergent, the outcome is always described in physical terms.

Those who remain spiritual spectators with good intent while devaluing anything physical as unworthy of spirit's proud notice have placed spiritual values at the wrong end of the telescope. It follows from this that those who are physically active—but of self-serving spirit—consistently gain control over what should be shared resources.

Spirituality is many levels of being below physicality; it is the sketch to the sculpture, the diagram to the machine, the plan to the journey. Regardless of how benevolent, any spiritual state first has a long way to go to fulfill its potential into materiality, whereas any physical act has already manifested it. The physical is the only place to prove that people who say that they practice the ideals of a spiritual life, actually do.

Without any material confirmation of a spiritual life, the result is what we see today: ever more cults and denominations whose only common factor is their claim to the truest life of the spirit and beyond. The extent to which claimants will go to insist on the superiority of their way climaxes in a contest between would-be rulers of the Universe, all using spiritual words to justify horrendous actions against others.

The meek shall inherit the earth, but not its mineral rights. J. Paul Getty, Businessman

---

For the spiritually well intentioned among us, it is not enough to claim that we are spiritual; we must actualize our spiritual ideals into physicality in whatever way is open to us. Since actions must start their journey in seed form, we all have a default spiritual life and do not need to go in search of one.

The theme of how to have a benevolent spiritual life is best framed around the question: "What are the character traits worth cultivating?" The answer depends not upon culture or belief systems but upon their effects, which will have the same value everywhere. The list includes sincerity, honesty, patience, understanding, courage, responsibility; and many others.

As a consequence of developing such qualities, ideal directions and opportunities in one's life will appear on their own because such spiritual assets create the optimal environment for life to flow and to network. A benevolent spiritual life is the foundation of a sublime adventure whose potential exists within all. However large or small our life's garden, it only awaits the nurturing of our carefully selected spiritual seeds for its optimal harvest.

23

REAL GOOD

IN THE CONVENTIONAL SENSE, TO "BE GOOD" describes a desirable character trait that supposedly, benefits both others and ourselves. Quite the contrary; the great flaw of being *good* is the contrast that it needs between its presumed superior worth and *bad's* equally presumed worthlessness.

For every bright, good form that we create we must simultaneously create a dark, bad one. As a result, when we want to appear good to others we must force our behaviour into a "good enough" form—whether it is the best one either now, or in the long run. Even worse, though "good form" implies a good content, it does not guarantee it. Instead, it becomes a façade behind which we are discouraged to look, lest in doing so we were already acting badly.

Good form's inevitable credit-line facilitates both corruption and easy deception because it does not demand that the presumed good content simultaneously reveal itself along with it. Form alone is then both the promise and its fulfillment, rather than simply its potential as a threshold. Many people become so mesmerized into presenting a good enough form that they lose sight of the obligatory content at the heart of that form's value.

"Being good" also sets standards of behaviour that are determined by an external authority rather than by our own conscience; life's least corruptible judge. Consequently, to insist on *appearing* good accumulates impurities that would naturally dissipate if given a way out of our system. "Looking good" thus leaves our native reflexes locked into the potentially "bad" character that "good" needs for its own ballast. Consequently, many people are so afraid to look at what might be "bad" in them that they never let their being do its natural self-cleaning.

Rather than lowering ourselves to the hollow standard of being good, we are best off being real, which happens when a form accurately points to its contents—regardless of what they are. To be real is therefore, more than good enough. It has to be, because our actual states of being are what shape our future, not our appearances or superficial behaviours. By being real we also synchronize with what we're broadcasting into the environment; a silent message that others sense at some level in their being. This awareness cannot be avoided because at deep enough strata, we all merge into a unity of shared information.

It is not so much the nature of what is real that is most important, but the fact that its authenticity can be firmly factored into our perceptions. This reliability spares us the work of having to second-guess the true relationship between a form and its contents, as well as any sense that something is "off" in what we are being shown. Instead, we have the same kind of perceptual certainty that numbers offer: we can count on our conscious perceptions and latent impressions. As a result, we can be both spontaneous and self-confident in our actions.

If we did not try to create any good in us at all, but quality of character instead, then each could stand elevated without first needing to lower another, given that authentic goodness comes in many forms and on a case-by-case basis. Qualities other than goodness are worthy of our cultivation and actually lead to what goodness is supposed to be about, but without requiring the duality of good vs bad. To name only a few: *understanding, compassion, transparency, sincerity, responsibility, honesty, self-initiative*.

With such standards as the constellations by which we navigate, our conscience is free to be the impartial loom upon which we weave ourselves out of ever-finer threads of being. It will do so in ways that inevitably materialize into real goodness.

24

Prove My Faith

Christians tweet more happily, less analytically than atheists.[88]

Whether believers realize it or not, if their faith does not deliver concrete proof of its validity then there will always be a degree of doubt somewhere within them. No person's neurology can insert certainty and trust into their faith without external evidence of its truth. In proof's absence, faith can only go so deep, which sometimes is enough for the challenges one encounters in a lifetime. Even if it is untested, faith can still offer us companionship and reassurance.

The internal dilemma only comes when our faith must be applied to situations that are so contradictory, so illogical, and so fantastic that the believer must turn off their intellectual processes to continue holding onto their faith. Under those circumstances, if they want to preserve it then a believer needs to firewall themselves against doubts and suspicions. The result is a neurological compartmentalization around which they must go, and whose boundaries must not be crossed. Additionally, a sense of passivity sets in and any options to change the situation are abdicated because one cannot think of them in a methodological way.

In contrast, proof-based faith consolidates itself through promises made actual and instills a faith-forward expectation that one's beliefs are true-to-life. Consequently, nothing in the believer's nervous system and consciousness need ever be quarantined from any other part. The effect is that their experiences can flow throughout all areas of their being rather than in some but, especially not in others.

As touched upon previously, "sense " is an important aspect of any information, religious or otherwise, because it represents reassuring orientation at core biological levels. As it does for all wild animals, "sensing" leads us to feel the universe's ground under our feet, with all directions properly positioned in relation to one another. Without such sensory orientation, there is "non-sense" and we cannot act with a sure footing.

Faith therefore, is most deep and powerful when it makes sense, and when it comes after proof rather than without it. With proof in the rear-view mirror, there is neither hesitation nor stagnation in our overall neurological flow. As a result, no energy is spent to silence misgivings. Instead, there is profound trust, certainty of action, enthousiasm, and confidence–all of which are at risk of being lost from unproven belief systems.

The thing that makes unproven systems seem true nonetheless, is blind faith's effect upon our brain: namely, that of isolating the activities of our left and right brain hemispheres. In general, any faith is processed through the holistic nature of the right hemisphere, a part of the brain that cannot readily express why it acts and perceives as it does. Only the strong analytical and textual capacities of the left hemisphere can explain and evaluate the basis for a set of beliefs. For this, it needs proofs to first convince itself, then you.

Blind faith arises simply from the imperative "you must believe" and has no separate text of reasoning to accompany it. Since it cannot offer material for the left hemisphere to process, it leads to the default isolation of the right one. With such a hemispherical isolation and separation there is no possibility of engaging in a logical discussion as to the why or how of one's beliefs. Within many belief systems, and ingeniously so through religious doctrines that frame any doubts as the sign of an insincere believer, the left hemisphere is actively discouraged from participating in one's faith. All the while, oblivious to the catch-22 of this framing, the wordless right hemisphere simply accepts what is. [89]

If the critical and analytical left's participation were mandatory for an exercise of faith, then so would a logical cause & effect explanation. No faith could then implant itself without solid evidence that its associated belief system represented true-to-fact phenomena. However, without concrete markers to examine its viability, anything at all can be accepted based on faith alone.

Deep faith without proof is often the default setting when small children are indoctrinated into a belief system, well before their cognitive development is complete. Because an infant's left hemisphere is not yet sufficiently informed to analyze any belief system, this early involvement is a de facto separation of the left and right hemispheres.[90]

"God doesn't want to be analyzed," one woman explained to me. "He wants your love." [91]

For those whose faith is deep, there will always be a way to accept just about everything within their belief's paradigm. No matter what happens, they are going to tap into the inherent malleability of reality, whose pliability allows for the validation of any belief that is sufficiently fueled by emotions and imagination. Deep faith is precisely what catalyzes a true believer's imagination to draw out, not a logical but a meaningful explanation for what happens to them, even when it involves dramatic loss and distress. Most of us have heard the phrase "It's God's will".

Given that life's major creative thrust is that of variations on a theme, there is no initial problem in the fact of different religions and belief systems. Blind faith's global hazard is that it inevitably leads to conflicts between belief systems that make dramatic–if not deadly–confrontations inevitable because any faith that rests on belief alone is equivalent to every other belief-based one.[92]

The drawback of blind faith at the individual level, is that we end up accepting limits and conditions that we could do without, or wish we didn't have to deal with at all. In contrast, precisely because it has proven itself, the proof-based faithful can use their whole faith to develop their potential and do so without friction or second-guessing the dialogue between their heart and mind.

It is up to each person to find that threshold beyond which they cannot continue to act on unproven faith. For some, this point is never reached because their faith directs doubts into a specific role such as: "My faith is being tested, therefore I must increase it." Such blind faith still constrains the believer at deeper levels of being. Only concrete proofs that validate our metaphysical beliefs will allow us to act with the boldness that the deepest certainty brings to any actions and goals.

Trust in the authenticity of our beliefs is particularly important for the concept that we can each transform our experiences of reality. Without proof, faith in this paradigm is especially absurd since there is no point in believing that you can transform reality yet all the while, everything stays the same.

How many opportunities to prove itself must we give the concept that we can direct our own life story? Each person must determine these limits for themselves. Often though, there comes a time when we want to abandon waiting for proof, for it somehow seems overdue. And yet, there is an urge to persist and to give it just one more chance. It is usually at this 11th hour when proof appears, thanks to which our faith is strengthened for even more ambitious projects.

Being a scientist, Hawking has faith only in scientific explanations. Instead, he thinks: "We are the product of quantum fluctuations in the very early universe." [93]

As we regularly see proofs of desired changes in our lives, we increasingly feel a sense of universal support. It is at this point when we realize that we can afford to live according to our most cherished ideals and goals. Consequently, we begin to live life as a high art form, one in which we have nothing to prove to anyone but ourselves.

25

W / INNER

The great thing in all education is to make your nervous system your ally instead of your enemy.
William James, Psychologist

WHATEVER SOCIETY YOU LIVE IN, the conventional way to increase your options and status is to obtain an education, one whose contents is determined by your society's culture. To know how to make a fishing net won't help you much in Manhattan, but it does when you live in a New Guinea tribe.

This is one form of education, but to be truly educated is to understand the nature of reality and what we can do within it. This requires us to learn about life's forces, to identify and recognize them, and then to know how to use them in service of our wellbeing.

To recognize and understand the major forces at play within ourselves is an ongoing process, and one that graduates us into ever wiser self-management. It is based upon our freedom of thought and our sharpness of perception, which can only come from direct engagement with life itself, and not by way of virtual events extracted from books and screens.

What external schools offer us are only maps and tools for the external world, whereas life's predominant territory is found within us and not outside–as schools train us to believe. Whether your education comes from an elite school or consists of street smarts, no outer education can compensate for the neglect and lack of collaboration with one's inner world. Consequently, regardless of the kinds of diplomas that we obtain, if we have not yet studied and inhabited our own inner world, then we're only half educated.

> *"We focus on the outside world in education and don't look much at inwardly focused reflective skills and attentions, but inward focus impacts the way we build memories, make meaning and transfer that learning into new contexts."* [94]

Whereas an inner education automatically expands to include an external one, the reverse is not true. Traditional educational systems keep us so focused upon outer information that, short of a crisis, we never prioritize developing our inner life. This skewed emphasis neglects how our inner and outer worlds are interdependent and entangled. Outside is not apart from inside, but an extended expression of it. In parallel, the inside is continuously stimulated and reconfigured by what appears outside.

A relationship with our inner world is a better teacher for learning how to develop our external potential than any scholastic life plan. Within each of us there is access to a vertical depth of field that provides real-time insight and guidance for our activities at exterior levels and their various timelines.

The deeper the levels of being that we reach for, the closer we come to the "seed" realities that are taking on materiality. This proximity to pure energy's instructions lets us reach any goal with fewer outer actions. Such deeply rooted guidance is essential if we want to actualize our lives from a position of freedom and effectivity.

The inner world is such a good mentor because its collaboration flows to us as our birthright, which logically enough, is to be full of life. Its mentoring speaks to us through the language of feelings, insights, thoughts, and through direct prompts into any actions that serve our boldest goals. Our inner senses can even reach into the future to guide us through what is in the offing around the corner.

Since they reconnect us full circle to our source, our inner world's activities are forms of pure religious practices that function to actualize our deepest needs and wants. As far as we know, the etymology of the word *"religion"* describes the action *"to bind" "to fasten"*. It is formed from the Latin *"ligere"*, the same root used for "ligaments." The prefix *"re"* relates to *"again,"* as in: *re*connect, *re*member.

As with any religion, a connection to our source only takes place through a passageway created with our own being and no one else's. By taking responsibility for our self-actualization we can always be located where every religion strives to be but can never reach without our deepest permission: namely within us.

If we leave it solely to an institutionalized religion to monitor our inner world then we will feel that we must behave according to its beliefs, and not according to our inherent compass. As a result, we might spend much of our time and energy comparing what we *should* be doing with what we actually *are* doing. Moreover, the standardized elements of most religions dictate that its dogmas be addressed to a generic human being and not to anyone in particular—you or me, for example.

Such a fixed approach is guaranteed to cut off those parts that spill over its templates, like dough beyond the edges of a cookie shape. Doctrines both idealize and demonize us; they create demands that exceed what most of us can deliver, and usually more than we should have to.

This viewpoint does not dismiss the role of any religion itself, but highlights the difference between exploring your inner world on your own, or else following a self-proclaimed guide to a place that they can never reach—your deepest self.

To use our inner world as an existential workshop is one of the most pragmatic things that we can do. This space is the only one where we can align with life according to our individuality and within conditions specific to our life story. Our tools are: reflection, analysis, meditation, self-inquiry, and others. These processes of inner connection guide us towards the fulfillment of our needs as unapologetically as a tree is primed to absorb nutrients from the ground around its roots.

The source of our existence recognizes that human yearnings extend into the shifting landscapes and objects of a socialized world, and not just to a level of basic sustenance. Simple survival is only the starting point of our lives and once this is provided for, our thirsts for human roles, experiences, and environments, arise and seek relentlessly to quench themselves.

We humans need to have our emotional, psychological, intellectual, and creative potentials satisfied to their optimal levels. In its awareness of this, the source of our being delivers to us a range of resources that nourish us in all aspects.

The alternative to this deep authenticity is to sail through life without a rudder, the consequence of which is that we drift according to each moment's strongest influence. This force will naturally shift with every new set of circumstances and participants. However, with our self-determination we can instinctively sense our way into building the life that we envision, regardless of complications and always with life's participation as our strongest ally.

The supposed fixed state of what is called "reality" is a misinformation whose influence comes from our conventional education's convincing bias towards the external world and its components. By their infinity of potential combinations, outer elements give an impression of universal dominance, the collective of which can overshadow the contents of one's inner world.

As mentioned elsewhere in this text, the appearance of inviolate laws of physicality is an essential, but ultimately deceptive device. Its twist is that, to get the full kick out of any experience, reality must feel *as if* it had no choice but to be as absolute as it appears to be.

Without this illusion of something's concrete being there would be no edge to its presence. Nothing would really matter after all, and so all the tension between us and what is would droop like a loose guitar string—and all the potential for music along with it. There could be no storylines without such constraints, no distinct objects, no trans-generational histories: in other words, no process or growth.

Unlike the outer-world, the inner one has no such restrictions of scale and time. It lets us move in ways that can dispense with reason, measurement, linearity, and justification. Moreover, also unlike the outer one, it is our own domain at every instant.

To appropriate this landscape begins our partnership with the power of information. Together, we become co-creative with the crossfield, a womb that incubates into life whatever our imagination and feelings seed it with—for better, or for worse. Deliberately directing this world's contents is as important as responding to the outer one because what is going on outwardly is a direct reflection of our inner resonances. Smooth these out, and what manifests must improve.

This dynamic is unfailing, and the basis for its synchronicity comes from the virtual nature of our experiences. Every instant of reality is the material translation of vibratory patterns whose information we first process from within. The tonal forms of our private topologies are why awareness of our feelings is essential for a purposefully directed life.

Unless we acknowledge how we are feeling at any given moment, we cannot realize the affirmative correlation between how we feel and the realities that we are subsequently forced to navigate.

It bears repeating: feelings are the 1-Dimensional form of what might develop into a 2nd, 3rd, and then 4th dimension. Like train wagons hitched to one another, with each feeling we contact vibrational textures that draw the next experience of feeling from which, once again we anticipate yet another tangible materialization, and so the ride continues. Feelings matter because—justified or not—they predict future sensory information, be it desired or feared.

Since what we each label as important is personal, to follow our feeling-links customizes our experiences as no external educator can. The very essence of teaching is in fact, to increasingly refine someone's nervous system into sophisticated perception and understanding. These then foster evermore effective actions; no one can teach us faster or more deeply than we ourselves.

When we first enter our inner world from the vantage of an "I" looking at itself, we generally still act as if our identity were our whole self. Our inner world, however, oscillates between individuality and universal oneness. In order to be fully partnered with it, we have to remember that "I" is a temporary crystallization of forces pretending to be a single being and that our complete self is an extension of the totality of being.

Before long, the inner world's vast territory will be understood as the prerequisite for a full education. There is already increasing information about the inner and outer world's primary instrument of receptivity and transmission: the brain. The more its functioning is known, the more obvious it will be that emotions, thoughts, feelings, and personal attitudes are our shapers. Their roles will be clear in not only what a person perceives and does, but also in what they cannot perceive, and cannot do.

The clear majority of people will tell you that there is no way that they (or you) can transform reality from within. Nevertheless, there is no need to convince others that reality is malleable for this concept's transformative effects to work for us. All we need to do is educate ourselves about our own inner and outer lives, and watch our self-directed changes unfold, as they must.

26

Form, the Universal Factor

The paradigm of an organic self is framed within the viewpoint that our reality is transformable to the point of literally being an art form, which is to say: a creative activity in which we can become skilled.

The more we practice reacting to circumstances based upon this premise, the more we will get proof of our creative control. To that end, it is far more effective to think about reality's contents in terms other than its meaning or identity; to think initially in terms of its *form*.

If you spend a little time thinking about it, you'll note that all things exist in some distinct form or other, whereas meanings and identities vary. Form's universality is a cure-all for enabling agreement when meanings differ. We can readily concur on the form of something (i.e.: as a thought, a feeling, an object, a fantasy, etc.) even when we cannot agree on its semantic value, its meaning.

Indeed, form is a universal factor, and a beautiful one at that for its constancy amid ongoing changes. Though each form varies, it remains constant as a form of some kind.

Since each form engages our physical apparatus in a different way, the fundamental question of any reality is not: "is it real?" but rather: "what form does this reality have?" The answer automatically lets us know the forces and dimensions involved and therefore, what our options are in relation to it.[95]

Is the form physical, as with an external object and so, potentially shareable? Is it conceptual, as with a thought or idea, and so a question of understanding the words used to describe it? Alternatively, is it emotional as with feelings, and so a question of managing and interpreting one's own neurology?

Whatever dimensionality the form might take, its role is to convey information about its being. In life, as in television, we are mesmerized into thinking that separate things are going on when instead, everything is happening on a unified screen—in the case of reality, that screen is activated by information. We know that on a monitor there is a technique being used: the activation of multiple meaningless points of energy: pixels. The physical dimensions that seemingly arise from the screen are illusions, and very effective ones.

This is possible because each disinterested, but specifically constructed, point on the screen plays its part towards the goal of presenting an impression of reality. All the while, it exists with no greater identity than that of a single generic point. In the same way as those pixels on a screen, our perceptions are the composite of our senses' activities energized by the information that they process.

Information combined with perception and imagination shapes our nervous system, which in turn, informs our subsequent perceptions and imaginations. Due to this cause and effect relationship, we can transform our reality through the information that we allow to influence our neurology. We can identify the state of our synaptic activity by observing our thoughts, feelings, and actions.

The stem *form* in "in**form**ation" is what we recreate with our imaginations, something that we have already been primed to receive via the word's prefix *in* (**in**formation). Finally, its suffix *ion* (informat**ion**) ionizes our nervous system into any one of its 3 possible states: activated, inhibited, or unchanged.

Information is the natural medium for the content of our experiences—it is a way of establishing the forms that are involved in each reality. Whatever the situation at play, feeling good is the key sensory information that we will seek out. We will usually accept the form in which good feelings arrive, just as long as they do appear.

Meet Some of the Form Family

Information
Misinformation
Transform
Platform
Reformation
Deformation
Formalize
Formless
Informal
Nonconforming
Perform
Unformed
Inform
Misinform
Formation
Transformation
Reform
Deform
Formal
Formidable
Formula
Conformity
Uniform
Uninformed
+ dozens more [96]

27

THE MENTION OF DIMENSIONS

Force: the ability to effect something on one's own terms.[97]

"TO BE" IS TO APPLY OUR OWN forces amid other equally self-affirming ones. How a being responds to forces and exercises its own will determine the reality that it cannot help but experience.

Everyone reading this text was forced into being through structural information—at a minimum, that of chromosomes and of literacy. According to the terms of its own informational blueprint, the universe was also forced into being.

Such is the nature of life that anything can be made to exist when the necessary informational forces and materials for its creation can be combined. Moreover, any being will last as long as it is not subject to another force that can deconstruct it.

Creativity in action is the most powerful force we have for our personal use. It, and not consciousness, is the defining characteristic of a human being. Whereas all that exists has its own form of consciousness, not all beings can rapidly create new things. Humans can.

Our species is constantly increasing its options by disassembling and reassembling as much of the world as possible. The result is that we can free ourselves from the context in which a force operates on its own terms and make it instead, serve our purposes. This dynamic is the basis for all technology and design. Our own life forces consistently shape us in response to our feelings and to our ideas. It is their implied longings that become the emotional instructions which then direct virtual particles of energy into materiality, either with our participation or by default.

Regardless, the form of whatever reality materializes always has a degree of dimensionality to it, from 0 to 4 dimensions:

0-Dimensions - The crossfield of being (Source); which contains all the structural concepts needed to direct undifferentiated energy into full 4-Dimensional presence.

1-Dimensional - Feelings, the pre-verbal sensing of information through our contact with the 0-Dimensional vibratory landscape from which 4-Dimensional objects and events can arise.

2-Dimensional - Words, Images.

3-Dimensional - (Inner) imagination: it adds a dimension of change to the 2D of images and words.

3-Dimensional - (Outer) something still with 3 spatial dimensions (height, width, length.)

4-Dimensional - Something with the 3D of outer spatial dimensions to which is added the process of its changes, which we frame as time.

28

Mass Appeal

It isn't too late. I can still back out...[98]

Just as the mass of the moon influences the tides of the earth, so does the mass of those beings that we encounter exercise their pull upon us. To the degree that we take them seriously, all things have a tangible psychological mass that compels us to be in a relationship with them, be they concepts, objects, people, situations, thoughts, feelings, and anything else that you can relate to.

The mass in question is not from something's size, but from the existential pull that we associate with it. Water, for instance, wets us wherever it is. However, getting wet in the Mediterranean during a stay at a luxury hotel has a completely different psycho-emotional profile than does getting wet during a flood.

The mass of anything first depends upon its role in our survival at some level or other, from spiritual, to emotional, to social, to imaginary. According to which level a thing has the potential to impact—favourably or unfavourably—to that extent we are either drawn into its mass, or else seek to distance ourselves from it.

Each mass' effect will continue until we or something else exerts a counter-active force. Something's mass can be unique to us due to our own thoughts and feelings—as is the case with passions or phobias—or it can come from cultural evaluations such as: status, authority, tradition, taboos, appearance, and so on.

The larger a thing's mass, the more we are pulled along the lines of its own forces. This attraction is based as much upon a thing's inherent importance (air, for example) as it is upon our assumption that something *is* important, even if upon subsequent examination it may not actually be so.

Advertising, for instance, always seeks to maximize the mass of its messages in order to trigger us into exchanging its object's mass for our money's—whose mass has already been agreed upon (the more money, the greater the mass). Effective advertising draws us in; we often just gravitate around it while we decide if we are going to let ourselves go. When we pull away, then our motives for not buying have the greater mass.

A mass' attraction can also come from its potential to reduce or remove an existing mass whose effect on us is oppressive. If we are lost in the desert, a glass of water has huge mass; when in a bar, the alcoholic drink has the greater draw and water may not even be noticed.

One key to our existential liberation is to question and deconstruct the basis for anything's mass. Otherwise, if we do not interrogate a seemingly strong mass then by default, we remain passive in relation to its pull. By contrast, an internal process acts as a brake and counterforce that permits us to move more freely around a given subject matter, and to evaluate for ourselves if its mass is warranted or if it is simply inflated.

Often, we are drawn unawares into situations and values whose masses come from their own self-promotion. The strength of such attractions convince us that certain ideas, obligations, people, conventions, rituals, etc., are important, even urgent. Consequently, we unquestioningly stay within their orbits; we also feel acute discomfort when we try to pull away. In cultures that cultivate group conformity, the more independently spirited individuals might well experience significant guilt when they want to distance themselves from the group and its influence over them. As a result, it is often necessary for such individuals to go to extremes in order to "snap" out of it.

Sometimes a subject's mass is the natural result of our relationship to it, as with family members, some of whom have so much mass that they pull on us throughout our entire lives. This is especially true when it comes to one's immediate family. The fact that there is only one degree of genetic difference between them and us gives their existence great density.

It looks as though it is a good idea for less powerful parties to negotiate from remote locations rather than face-to-face. When people negotiate from further apart, it affects their whole way of thinking. ”

Our interactions with anything's mass leads to the following principle: right relationship is based on right distance. We determine the ideal space between a subject's mass and ourselves according to the level of our comfort or discomfort.

A comfortable feeling leads us to want to come closer still, and we'll probably do so until we are once again in a place of excessive pressure. Conversely, when we are distressed by our closeness to a given mass then we'll want to get further away, if we can.

Depending upon the kind of relationship that it is, we can be in a process of constant adjustments, towards and away from something or someone. The "right distance" principle is why we can more readily forgive people over time or after their deaths. In each case, our distance from them increased and so, their masses and effects decreased.

Although distance from anything affects how much gravity it has for us, a thing's mass also depends upon our underlying ideas as to who and what we are in relation to it. To be aware of these premises we have to follow the trail of a subject matter's formulations about reality and self. The more complete this investigation, the broader will be our understanding of the root concepts at play, and the easier it becomes for us to be in touch with our own thoughts and feelings on a given matter.

If in fact a mass turns out to be of no consequence to us, then this realization alone is enough to thrust us away from what previously drew us in. Either that, or we recognize its actual importance and so, can accept our attraction to it. Once we see the masses at play, we also realize the action or non-action needed for our right relationship to them; this is when the dynamics of fun can come in.

29

FUN

And she'll have fun, fun, fun 'til her daddy takes the T-Bird away ~ ~ ~ The Beach Boys

---

IF WE LOOK TO SEE WHAT MOST people want to do, we'll see that having fun is close to the top of their list. The U.S. Constitution, written in 1776, already recognizes this fact with its inclusion of "the pursuit of happiness" as one of the top three human rights that a government is meant to protect, just after "life" and "liberty".

The experience of fun doesn't necessarily come from the specific activity itself, but because of the freedom from gravity that it offers. Fun lets us put aside all kinds of information that would otherwise weigh upon us, given that to be able to discount information liberates us from its demanding effects upon our actions, psychology, and nervous system.

Fun happens when the mass of an idea or an action is reduced, eliminated, or naturally light. The common thread is an absence of neurological activity connected to meanings that are more serious, and thus, have more mass. As a result, we can be light-hearted and enjoy direct sensory contact with the fun activity itself. Contrary to its image, fun is not automatically a benign enterprise; one person's fun can be another person's distress, as in the case of criminality.

As described in the last chapter, every situation and subject matter has a basic mass at several levels. Sometimes the mass comes from the essential role of the thing itself, as in the importance of air for breathing; anything that cuts off our air supply is never fun. When we are underwater with an air tank, however, we can have fun because the conceptual mass of inaccessible oxygen is absent. At other times, we attribute mass to something specific, as in: "I've just got to have _______!" The ability to remove something's mass is key to the experience of fun. Mass can be reduced in various ways.

It's really fun and that makes it important to physicists. This is great physics – it's cute, it's fun, it's interesting.[100]

Skill makes the weight of an activity smooth and playful. Mastery means that we have enough expertise to make light of the materials and actions involved. Such an experience of competence is fun because we are no longer constrained by the weight of our awkwardness. We are also free from the gravitational pull of having doubts as to whether or not we are good or bad in our performance. Thus we literally can play with the forces of the materials involved.

Relief from responsibility leads to fun. An actual vacation—say, at a resort—is fun because we are free from the masses of work and domestic demands. We prime ourselves into this attitude by "being on vacation" and so giving ourselves permission to vacate any thoughts and feelings that have to do with responsibilities. As a result, we no longer have to respond to ordinary demands and can care only for our own pleasures.

The removal of significant consequences is fun, as in the playing of all sorts of games. Make believe and unrestricted spontaneous activities are enjoyable because the consequences of our actions are not intended to be meaningful—no significant neurology is engaged. This liberation from self-measurement does away with any judgments about how well we play or not: very young children clearly demonstrate this. Nonetheless, the eventual arrival on the scene of so-called "winners" versus so-called "losers" can add social mass to certain forms of otherwise inconsequential play.

Disregard for another person's rights feels like fun to certain personalities. Crime is often fun for the criminals—until they're caught and the gravity of the situation sinks in. Before that, there was great freedom from societal restrictions, imposed efforts, and postponed gratification.

Reduction in the semantic mass of words results in fun, as with humour and word play, which show us that no subject matter is sacred. Through a joke or cartoon, anything whatsoever can be made "light" of; only a person's own standards prevent them from going too far.

Once we experience relief from a subject matter's mass by laughter, it is difficult to return it to its previous heavier status. Hence the fanatic prohibitions of some belief systems to never make fun of them in any form whatsoever, or else... The threat serves to reintroduce the gravity that would otherwise be dissolved through the humour.

Chemical substances can reduce a person's sense of obligatory functionality and so, reduce the mass of things in general. The by-product is a sense of fun. The problem with this approach is that it can become very expensive in the long run as the masses of the neglected aspects of our lives return and oppress us into suffering. At that point, increasing amounts of chemicals are needed to return to the initial escape—whose original innocence is forever out of reach.[101]

Fun is essential. Without it, life becomes burdensome and

wears on our nerves with its constant demands to process conceptual and emotional loads. As a result, we infect others with the masses that we carry by passing them along and thus, reducing other's own capacity for fun. The ideal is to have on the one hand, just enough gravity so that what we do matters, and on the other, sufficient lightness of being to reduce our resistance to the guidance that is constantly flowing to us—inwardly and outwardly.

Fortunately, part of our human being-ness is that we have options for reducing the masses of our realities. Exercising these requires accepting concepts that correlate our external experiences with our inner activities. Otherwise, if we believe that reality comes at us strictly from the outside, then we must be ever vigilant in case something "heavy" is waiting around the corner. Consequently, we are never truly free to have fun or make light for very long.

However, if we realize that our reality is an extension of our self-directed imaginations, then we can give our full alertness and care to what is happening in our present moment where we can act in the now. As written elsewhere in this book, "now" is this most powerful of moments when all forces are aligned and steerable towards a desired state. Consciously directing these forces at their most potent confluence is to be in the "Now."

To think of our situations in this way increases our sense of control and reduces any urgencies we may feel to escape the moment. We then no longer need to act from purely external levels where random forces await us, but rather can act from a creative stance of drawing out the transformations that we need and desire.

This paradigm offers fun in the same way as a natural high. Lightness of being automatically arises when we are fully engaged in life at all levels: sensory, intellectual, emotional, physical, and spiritual. At such moments, we do not ask whether we deserve happiness or success, we simply sense that these vivid moments are what life is all about.

Such an intensely pleasurable state derives its effects from multiple sources of sensory information interflowing throughout our neurology. This unrestrained, all-inclusive joy is our most efficient way of being. It elicits the least amount of resistance to the moment and is in step with our greatest reach towards a global cooperation amongst the various forms of being that make up our individual and shared environments.

The thrust of a full life is exactly towards this intoxicating dynamic. It is one in which we are liberated from the gravitational pull of weighty matter and so, free to enjoy pure creative play in the moment. At that point, we are free to have all the fun that we can enjoy.

30

Art is About ~~Object~~ Process

To fulfill our creative potential, we must start by accepting the fact that by the very act of living we are already artists; we only differ in what we create: the life of an accountant, of a musician, of a librarian, of a mechanic, of a free-form artist. As we play out our life story, our ultimate creation is how we direct the forces and opportunities that arise each moment of the day.

Because transforming reality involves the exercise of our native creative skills, it is worth understanding the nature of creativity itself, something that is most evidently embodied in the role of those whom we call "artists".

These days, however, unless great sums of money are attached to them, no one can consistently identify who is or isn't a "real artist". Nor can anyone consistently tell us how to differentiate between "good" versus "bad" art–it's a matter of opinion. The origin of this fogginess is that after the 1900s the role of artists changed from having a specific representational skill to having the freedom to explore their materials and to engage in self-expression. The catalyst for this transformation was photography.

Before photography, every artist had to prove their ability to represent realistic or functional forms, either in 2 or 3 dimensions. The etymology of the word "art" shows its obligatory foundation of skill: *"art (n.) early 13th century, 'skill as a result of learning or practice.'"*[102] This pragmatic standard made it easy to know who was, or wasn't a real artist since, without ability you were unemployable, just as an untrained engineer would be today.

The word "artist" was also only an overall category for people who were specifically identified by the medium through which they exercised their skill: "painter," sculptor," "musician," "poet," "actor," or "dancer." Once the camera arrived, however, the artist's functional role changed rapidly and dramatically because early photographic chemistry produced images faster and far more exactly than any portrait or landscape painter could with canvas and pigments.

This technological advancement liberated visual artists to explore and deconstruct the various elements and materials of their craft. As a result, unhindered self-expression and experimentation increasingly became the main product offered by an equally expanding art market. Art critics, people self-appointed to tell the public what these free-range artists were doing exactly, further legitimatized the artists' internally guided output.

From the critics' opinions came labels for the various aspects supposedly explored by artists, i.e.: Impressionism, Futurism, Surrealism, Cubism, Abstract Expressionism, Conceptual Art, and others, with each movement going further and further away from classical forms. In the process, not only did the functional aspect of an art form disappear, but also the requirement for a concrete skill itself. In their place appeared the concept of creative expression.

And so, today, what defines an artist is whatever they do in the name of capital "a" "Art" without a companion term that identifies what skills of creation they have mastered. Nowadays, anyone can call themselves an artist, regardless of medium used or of aptitude on display. Consequently, so-called "important art" is measured in terms of its value in the marketplace; this amount then implies that there must be a skilled involved, or else why would it cost so much?

However, if you want to understand the actual art in something you first must identify the skill involved in creating the artwork, a skill that sometime resides only in the imagination of the artist, or of the beholder. At other times, the skill is as clear as it once was in the classical sense of being an artist, even though art media today might consist of concepts, social action, information, technology, performance, and whatever else an artist's imagination will conjure up.

Meanwhile, fine art's categorization as a high-end luxury artificially rarefies life's universal dynamic: creativity. The exorbitant price of some artworks is a further misdirection as to where the actual value of an artwork resides—and it is not in the object itself. The priceless part of any creation is the *creative process* by which it came to be, and every object, not just those identified as art, implies that such a process took place.

Because it disappears with each subsequent step, the creative process is something that only a self-aware creator can own. It is the source of an artist's greatest thrill, and one which goes beyond the joy that arises at the finished object, or even beyond the vast wealth that it may someday bring. In its presence as the submerged part of the art-object glacier, it is this implication of creative process that is the art buyer's primary purchase—a buyer who may themselves never experience it.

The irony of fine art's financial elitism is that the creative process is free and available to all who reach for it. Since striving for a skill is at the heart of every action, we are artists whenever we engage in the doing of anything, especially when we do so to the best of our ability, regardless of medium, from how we sweep a floor to how we perform surgery. Each life activity has its process that we can expand upon by sincerely getting into it.

Process is both king and queen; its vitality comes from how it forces us to negotiate our relationship with materials on their own terms. The result is that we experience only the pure fact of our being without any constraints of identity. It is within this space that we are free to explore the forces playing with us during a creative process, as well as exercising our own forces in dialogue with those of our materials.

The more we get into it, the more we are stripped down to our most transparent state of becoming, enabling all materials and forces to act out their mutually transformative potential. Our constantly refreshed insights then become the light that reveals the way for each next step. In this illuminated state we become naked being in combination with other pure beings. As our imaginations and feelings merge with the materials, all is discovery combined with forgetfulness of self. The surprises and mysteries on the way to the creative outcome is a uniquely intoxicating experience.

This wondrous activity is no different from what we did as children, at a time when it was easy to follow our own voice—the only one that made consistent sense, and whose initial influence never stops trying to express itself through us. Our inner voice is a permanently whispering self, and our dialogue with it is the beginning of a creative collaboration with our life force and its intended journey: a destination that is forever at the roots of our own existence. The deliberate education of our inner spaces gives this voice the recognition that it needs to take on increasing vigour. As our creativity finds ever more novel ways for us to actualize, our existential voice then reveals our truest self-expressions.

As an inherent part of life, the creative process runs its course with or without our conscious direction. However, only when we assert our own creative powers can we start to live with the same vitality as any animal in the wild, and do so in parallel with achieving socially driven goals. When undertaken with sincerity, we are neurologically different after a creative process from how we were at its beginning. Any artwork or life outcome is then only a by-product and not the main event.

That said, an art object implies and echoes its profound creative journey–to the point that creativity is one of the most highly prized human activities. The cost of a doctor who brings you back to life from the brink of death is far below that of a work by a renowned artist.

The Religion of Creativity

To enter the creative process is to take a path whose beginning and end rest on a spiraling curve, one whereby what has come into existence has fundamentally created itself through yet another aspect of its own being. With inspiration and imagination as its central drives, creation is an organic form of religion: universal and without hierarchy. A Creator, Creating, and the Created, are the trinity of collaborative dynamics whose bonded forces are all there is in life.

The thrill of any creative process is how it sweeps us into its currents and yet, accepts us as we are. It informs us that letting go is the way towards flow and lightness of being. In the same way that misaligned tubes cannot convey water, we sense that creative forces need our supple surrender in order to direct our internal alignment. In this state, we become shamanistic–we heal what needs to be whole by creating or restoring life anew.

The shaman's journey is very close to that of an artist's: both ways of being offer holistic action through transcendental processes. Ever since prehistoric times, as soon as undesirable conditions appeared, the quest began to find a cause. If it was not obvious, shamans were often called upon as transcendental agents of healing, and with them they sometimes brought what, today, we would call "art objects."

The created item represented a deep vibration of intention and was used as the portal for negotiations with healing forces.

Through such objects, sometimes accompanied by psychoactive substances, specific existential powers could be tapped into for shamanistic entry into fields of information and of transformation. This transcendental process required the shamans to offer their psyche to other influences, to be guided by them, and to interact with them on shared terms.

As a result, shamans experienced other levels of sensual information that existed simultaneously with so-called, ordinary life. This shamanistic venture required a self that could detach from social norms so as to achieve entry into an extrasensory wilderness, then reclaim itself upon return and reentry into society.

The shamanic process of tapping into deep forces of creation has not disappeared from modern life. We can each experience this exhilaration of creation's wild process without sacrificing the advantages of a sophisticated society. Whenever we exercise our inherent powers to create, to heal, and to effect changes in our and others' lives, we too act in a shamanistic-artistic capacity.

Every deliberate creation is itself a shaman's journey through varied states of being. Their dynamics engage us into a neurological activity whose pull is to disassemble our identity and its self-protections. In this way, we are stripped from conservative safety nets to better midwife the coming into being of a new creation, be it an object or our latest self-authenticity. Since such birth processes require us to be present in the moment, creating is among the most vivid adventures that life can offer.

Although exclusive art has its place, when we get rid of the idea that the only "real" art is what is expensive and museum-worthy, then we can live in terms of our own daily self-expression as the art form that it is. Our experiences will then naturally flow along the rivers of our passions; these always travel along our heartfelt energy's path of least resistance and so, that of its greatest efficiency.

31

Do Be Do Be Do

> *Someone in flow loses a sense of self-consciousness: the activity is entirely rewarding in and of itself, as one gains a sense of personal control over the activity.*[103]

We cannot create in an authentic way except by interacting with our inner being and letting go of our superficial social self. The singer of a song cannot expect to sing well because of their status, but from the quality of their vocals; chefs cannot prepare delicious meals because of the clothes that they wear, but only from their selection and handling of the ingredients; writers cannot write a compelling novel because of where they live, but because of their imaginations' contents.

A complete synthesis of both the doer and of the done offers an experience of being alive far beyond that of any successes according to social terms. No prize or public acknowledgment takes the place of an immersed doer who engaged in life-affirming animal immediacy.

To be is to do, and to fully "do" anything is to come under the influence of pure sensory information; to surrender into the done thing's own forces of being. We are now neither more nor less important than what is being done. We are, in fact, what is being done and nothing else. To be in a state of mind where you are pure being interacting with another pure being opens a process that spontaneously directs the doer into inspired actions, fresh ideas, insights, and overall pleasure. Our weightless being and resultant merger with the materials at hand becomes a thrilling liberation that leads us to our native creativity, which is always on hand to stream from within.

The more we view the contents of our moments as materials that are raw, freed from their context and liberated from their expected functions and meanings, the more intense and transformative the processes we can go through. This self-release allows the doing of anything to inform us as to its own needs for fulfillment, and it requires us to actualize our own authenticity.

Once we have gone through the creative process often enough, we recognize the empty space, the blank field from which we always begin any new action, any new thought, any new perception. We also understand that we can stop at midpoint, discard, and start anew—all without either a favourable or unfavourable significance associated with each fresh attempt. Instead, we willingly go back to zero, over and over again. Our mistakes do not feel as if anything went wrong; instead, what was just was, and what is just is.

This practice develops in us a capacity to be free from automatic and default meanings, not only in our actions, but also in relation to the concepts by which we live. As a result, we can glide through the moment and surf over ever more cresting self-expression. Since reality is itself a full-fledged medium, the transformations that come from experiencing our various creative processes also enhance our abilities to direct our life. It too can be creatively shaped and we do so at every instant, usually by default rather than with deliberation.

Nevertheless, to activate the dynamics necessary for self-directed transformations we need to merge our inner and outer spaces into a mutually aware whole. We also need to see our source state as pure energy, which is simply a blank page in another form. Such preparedness includes seeing all applications of language as art materials. Just as an author knows how each word shapes a developing story, so we form our own by how we tell it to others and first, to ourselves.

Those things that seem hard and inescapable have seduced us with their sensory play on our neurology. Their self-affirmed truths will insinuate themselves into our story until we challenge the premises of their texts about reality and about our control over it. Given that nothing anywhere is ultimately solid, no matter the tale told right now, it can be re-written for the better as well as for the worse.

Through the eager collaborator of our intentions and our access to internal guidance, we come to see the concepts and forces at play in our feelings, our thoughts, and our actions. Thanks to this overview, we have the inner space to determine which conceptual or emotional elements reduce us and which expand us, then know how to act accordingly.

Consequently, we no longer need to edit our life stories according to the dictates of socially shaped scripts. We now live with maximum authenticity—as wild animals already do. There is no limit to how much we can tap into this creative process. From it we can, literally, draw out a transformed life just as a line is drawn out of a pen.

32

TRUST ME

TRUST HAS THE DOUBLE-EDGED POTENTIAL to either take us to sublime levels of inclusion and intimacy, or else to open a trapdoor beneath our feet and swallow us whole. Sincere trust is illustrated in the unprotected belly of a kitten (a puppy...) waiting for our touch; with our trust in others, we too unguardedly offer them the most vulnerable parts of our nervous systems.[104]

From early on, we are taught to trust authority, especially those in the medical field, who are elevated to an almost "god-like" status. It is very easy for these individuals who are put in a position of power to take advantage of that power.[105]

The greater the trust involved, the vaster the area of the neurology that we are handing over. Because we have already surrendered the protection of many delicate and deep feelings is why it's painful when our trust in another person is betrayed at an intimate level.

The social constructs that surround us guarantee that we will be asked throughout the day to trust one another to varying degrees. The underlying assumption for trust in another person is that each one cares about their own integrity, just as you and I do. This is not always the case, and knowing whom to trust and when, is at the heart of a smooth emotional and social life. The delicate balance is to become neither so trustful as to trust universally, nor so skeptical as to trust no one, even when they deserve it.

The younger we are, the more readily we trust without hesitation; this is why children in their cognitive immaturity are inherently trusting. Their experiences of life are limited in both formation and information and, unlike adults, they do not know how to imagine what could go wrong.

In general, the easiest people to trust are those who are like us—however you define "us". Most societies have a built-in filtering system for identifying whoever belongs to their "in" or "out" groups. Those who can pass "in" have gone through some of the usual discriminating screens, such as: geographical origin, education, belief systems, politics, social class, income, diets, lifestyles, and others.

Stores of common experiences guarantee that among the members of any in-group there will be similarly configured neurological maps about various subjects and their individual values. Since agreement upon these promises consensus as to their protection, this concordance leads to a default state of trust. Nonetheless, group trust does not guarantee equally strong one-on-one trust among its members; that kind generally occurs on a case-by-case basis.

Our first encounter with a person or situation often triggers in us a gut-level sense for how much there is to trust. Unfortunately, we have usually been socialized so far from our uncorrupted and reliable animal natures that we do not even trust ourselves. Instead, we rely upon and defer to the subliminal idea-image values that we attach to a person's style, dress, status, and accompanying labels. Not only that, but simply by letting ourselves greet a person, we have already agreed to give them the benefit of the doubt, and so start to trust them.

The smaller the community in which we grow up, the more

likely we are to trust new people since we will have had a limited range of occurrences from which to have reasons for mistrust. By contrast, acting with blanket trust in a large city is predictably going to provide someone with an opening to abuse it. That is why visitors from smaller urban areas to larger ones are often easily taken advantage of. Meanwhile, the long-term urbanite's nervous system is constantly shielded—to the point that many live in a permanent state of skepticism as to any stranger's motives.

As a general principle, the more we must protect our nervous system from access, the more we will mistrust others and, as a side effect, the less we can conduct a fully open relationship with ourselves.

> *Mr. Falkner, 28, started it off by singing a song. New Yorkers' Pavlovian response to ignore kicked in: people continued to read, peer at their smartphones, sleep or listen to their own music.* [106]

DEGREES OF TRUST

The ultimate "prove it" distrusters are scientists; supposedly, they will not entrust their professional neurology to anything untested. This attitude is not maladaptive cynicism but instead, a mistrust of the unproven. The force that we give to a scientific statement comes specifically from our assumption that its conclusions originate from a consciousness with high standards for its trust in information. In a rather fair way, the sciences do not expect our trust until they have offered solid proof.

Unlike science, religions require an enormous amount of trust from their adherents since no belief system with words alone can prove that its cosmology is universally true. Religions must always lobby for our trust since they do not have a stand-alone product. As with any belief system, a religion is built upon the basis of a trust that may never have the opportunity to justify itself. Under such conditions, any proof as to a religion's "truths" can only occur inwardly on an individual level.

The collective nervous system of a society can also be described in terms of its trust quotient, which corresponds to the degree of trust that its members have in both its systems of government, and in one another. The more this trust is taken for granted, the more civilized is the society. Conversely, the more guarded and anarchic its members are, the less civilization a society can claim to have.

Since trust comes from the full delivery of information, what trust needs in order to be solid is indistinguishable from transparency—something also essential in relationship to our self. As the saying goes: "Ethical behavior is doing the right thing when no one is watching—even when doing the wrong thing is legal."

To act from a position that presumes all we do is eventually visible to some form of consciousness—if only our own—literally clarifies us to behave in ways that will be beneficial to all in the long run. This is not a rule to live by so much as a necessary element for a full life. Unless we act ethically in relation to ourselves and to others, we cannot trust anyone at those levels where trust makes a critical difference, such as a call to action vs non-action.

Interestingly, living with self-transparency has the same result as if we were being good on purpose, only without having to correlate our behaviour to a belief system for what good looks like in contrast to bad.

Instead, we can simply be as we are, without apology or justification. In that ongoing state we can trust ourselves, know whom to trust, and cannot help but inspire trust in others. What follows from this way of being is a natural internal alignment. At one end of it there is infinite access to the crossfield of being, and at the other, yet another present Now for us to experience and modulate. Once we see this mechanism flow, we can exercise the largest trust of all, which is that in life itself.

33

Words' Worth

Through the technology of words life literally takes on the ultimate form of high-definition. Defining their subject matter is what words do, as opposed to images, which illustrate. Words can either inform or misinform.

For them to be true, words must transport information that exists somewhere else as an actual entity. That is why a lie's reality exists only in the 2-Dimensional text of the words that it takes to say it—a lie has no 4-Dimensional presence elsewhere.

Based precisely on the words that we use to describe our life experiences to ourselves and to others, thus we seed and harvest the stories of our lives. As we magnify some elements and minimize others, this process makes editors of us all. From a structural point of view then, a lie is the ultimate form of editing.

Themomentiknew: He told me that he was going to visit his son but wore shorts & sandals on the plane. To New York. In December. Spockjones [107]

Regardless of its degree of truth, each word is a billboard that sells the supposed existence of its subject. As does any advertisement, it stands between us and what it indicates. In like fashion, any verbal descriptions of "my" life story will always be framed in a way that we each find most comfortable. A scene described by ten people will emphasize in every case those things that serve each person's self-preservation and status.

Separated by over a thousand years, the Bible and the Vedic texts both state that the "Word" was the beginning of life.[108] Whether as a metaphor or as a fact, that a word was the kick-start of existence makes complete sense because life is synonymous with information, be it via words or forms. When you can no longer receive information in any way at all, then you are no longer alive.

"Word" is also among the best of words to begin any story of genesis since it is one of the few that points back to itself. [109] Life begins by revealing its wit (what's another word for "word"?) However, life could have begun with any word since inherent in one of them is a system that needs a multitude of other words to accompany it.

Words are conceptual maps that reconstruct realities while they simultaneously unlock us from the linearity of time and the restrictions of distances. To the 2-Dimensionality of words, our imaginations add a 3rd animating dimension from the images that we associate with them.

Words cast spells that, literally, come from how words are spelled. We imagine far different realities when words write "they are poor" versus "they are rich." The very etymology of "grammar" takes us to the word "magic" and is also at the root of the word "glamor." [110]

The etymological echoes of words are keenly descriptive of a past made of tangible and dynamic materiality at many levels: physical, emotional, conceptual, and psychological. Many English words originated centuries back when being alive made great concrete and physical demands. Most people's everyday lives were then on a rough scale involving strenuous 4-Dimensional events.

Fast-forward to today's hyper-techno lifestyles where our vocabulary reflects words whose textures are slick, cool, and abstract. In opposite direction from pre-industrial times, these words reflect distances detached from human touch: nano, quantum, atomic, digital, satellites, software, memory, gigabytes, dark energy...

Oh dear, she wanted her hair dyed and now she's dying.[111]

Words are a human fabrication, and very word needs its author since no word can exist without first being thought of or spoken by someone. Interestingly, a word's popularity is then an organic exercise in democracy since each person votes for a word by electing to use it. On the elitist side, a rarely used word can become a finely meshed filter whereby only those who speak a given second language (for example, Sanskrit) or who know a specialized word (Sesquipedalian) can become part of a social or professional in-group.

There are thousands of languages and an infinity more can be created, but the things towards which any of their words point stay in the universe's most basic language, that of forms, of which there are several: material, emotional, conceptual, imaginary, etc.

Imagine a table where you eat. According to the language in which it occurs, the common spelling of the word for it will change: *Tavola, Tisch, mesa, tafel, tabela, sofra, tabl,* etc. Meanwhile, regardless of the different 2-Dimensional words by which your table is called, it stays constant in 4-Dimensionality as the physical surface that you know.

Paradoxically, within a given language, the 2-Dimensional form of the word "table" stays virtually the same. Again, meanwhile, the 4-Dimensional form of your table physically changes through the effects of usage: paint chips, knife cuts, oil stains, burn marks... Should we even think to mention these changes, we must still talk about the "table" using the exact same word each time.

As etymology shows us, words do not forever own their meanings. They only own the properties of their structural elements: written forms, translations, tonal associations, etc. Just listen to a language that you do not understand, or repeat a word over and over, and you will experience words as nonsensical vibrations represented by arbitrary shapes and lines. In the absence of literacy, no word's visual form or sound can reveal the reality that it is about; we have to be taught what a word represents.

The quality of our education correlates exactly to how well we understand the forces and forms that a given word designates, and in what context.

Professor Moriarty: "Put those tools away until they're needed!"
Dr. Onslow: "But they're not tools, Sir, they're instruments." [112]

In all cases, our personal knowledge of words increases our perception and our mastery over situations. Each person can alter the social and personal levels of power available to them simply by learning specific words and when to apply them.

The more culturally refined one is, the more words one has for seemingly, the same object. A glass is then not only that, it is specifically a "water glass," a "red wine glass," (differentiated into Bordeaux or Burgundy), a "white wine glass," a "beer glass," a "champagne flute," a "sherry glass," a "smoothie glass," and so on...

The irony of this verbal refinement is that brute physicality might still have the last say. No words hold us back when our immediate security or long-term survival is threatened. Champagne flute in the way or not, we make a mad dash to leave as soon as we hear the word "Fire"!

This fact highlights how our modern luxuries and capacities are only extensions of life's primary motivators: to survive, then to create—in the case of humans, especially for creation's sake. In the process, what we invent begs for new words to also be created.

All words are equally true in their fundamental emptiness since there is no master word for anything. What is the "real" word for something when it sounds and looks different according to the language? Only what it is pointing to stays as what it is—even if not everyone's perception of it is the same.

He gathered over 1,100 words for "banana" from indigenous languages throughout the islands of Southeast Asia. [113]

Words can be more accurately understood when viewed as 2-Dimensional graphics than as meanings. Words have form, just as form is itself a language. To see a word without first coming under its spell requires us to consider its elements in a purely visual way. It also requires the ability to read form as a language all its own. As concretely as words, the language of form contains information that distinguishes each thing from every other.

A form's definition is built from a multitude of parts. To name a few: its geometric properties, its capacity for reorientation (circles roll, lines don't), the character of its angles (open, sharp), its symmetry (or not), the wavelengths of its colours (warm to cool), the cultural context of its parts (symbolism), its materials (metal, concrete, smoke), its mobility (stable, erratic, slow, fast, moderate), its size (small to large), its visibility, its location (inside or outside), its tactile textures (smooth, rough,) the means by which it comes into being (e.g. metal, driftwood,) and many other sensory aspects that have nothing to do with meaning, but with sensory information.

With rather poetic justice, just as words affirm realities, they can also undo them. The conceptual basis of our life allows for a complete reformulation of our perceptions simply through a change of words in how we describe them ("I am worried" versus "I am concerned.") Before we can rephrase any story, however, we must disassemble the one that exists. This process requires us to view a situation's meaningful (to us) subject matter in its most fundamental form: as pure energy that is vibrationally guided by our emotions and concepts—especially those regarding self and reality.

Vibrations, either in the air or in our minds, are the basic bodies of the words that we use and that use us. Similarly, our bodies are both structured and de-structured via vibrations, including those of words—a fact that leads medical technology to come ever closer to using pure vibrations as a means to influence the organizational forces in our bodies, and therefore our health.

This is why the words of our affirmations have the potential to create changes, including great ones. Specific word combinations—spells, so to speak—have the potential to catalyze beneficial structures and relationships within our organism; they can even lead to epigenetic changes. Our use of affirmations not only benefits us, but also has the potential to advance the entire human species through a conceptual investment forward.

The power of words to both build up &/or to disassemble perceptions makes many life solutions possible. As a chemist uses this word, *a solution* represents a mixture of materials in suspension, and not yet settled into their lowest and most stable level. This definition describes how we can process the words we use to deal with problematic conditions, thoughts, and feelings: we can stay in suspense as to their final state, all the while keeping an optimal outcome steady in our vision.

Words are the epitome of domesticated creatures. If they turn on us, it is because we have stressed them by our reactions to their imposed meaning. Only when we see their fundamentally passive nature can we dispel the power of any words used to oppress and intimidate us, including when we use them to discourage ourselves.

Because our thoughts, feelings, ideas, reflections, etc., are all formalized through language, we need both kinds of relationships to words—trust in what they can offer, and a detached analysis of how they exercise their effects upon us.

34

KINDS OF MEANINGS

PART I

" You" your choice and your sorrows, your memories and your ambitions, your sense of personal identity and free will are in fact no more than the behavior of a vast assembly of nerve cells and their associated molecules.
Francis Crick, Co-Discoverer of the structure of DNA[114]

MEANINGS WEAVE THEMSELVES INTO our perceptions as if meaning itself were something external and inevitable. However, meaning is not inherent to life, but a powerful act of human creation, one that comes from within.

You cannot physically locate another person's meaning, nor hand over your own; meaning can only be transmitted via self-expression and its reception. When this is successful, the receiver can "try on for size" the subject matter's neurological networks within the sender, enough so to have a sense of what is meant.

This kind of receptivity to another's way of interpreting life is at the roots of such experiences as realization, understanding, insight, empathy, and true communication. When this fails, however, then misunderstanding another's meaning can readily lead to aggression and conflicts of varying degrees. This battle can be framed as: my nervous system is right and yours is wrong. The error here results from how easily we can agree on obvious physicality in the outer world and assume from such shared views that we all see the same meanings in them as well.

However, our inner world is where meanings arise, for the outer world is without them. It only contains specific forms, textures, processes, and forces, something that any animal can recognize and respond to. Wild animals routinely respond to their environments based on how they experience it sensorily and in the moment, but not according to meanings. Most animals will infer intrusion from the occurrence of a sudden loud noise, or imminent change from a fast movement nearby. Sensory information of this kind is always about something concretely based.

When someone says that they "really mean it," and they do, then you can be sure that their whole nervous system is engaged in the materialization of their expression. The counterpart of "I didn't really mean it," represents that their actions were based upon weather of the moment, and not on any deep neurological commitment to the message itself.

The word "mean-ing" is an extension of the term "mean" that we encounter in mathematics where it is used to describe the average measure for a range of something's possible values.[115] Similarly, the meanings that we ascribe to experiences, things, words, etc., come from their average values as added by each of our nerves' neurochemical accounting.

The reverse engineering of meaning's neurological structure is: change what something means and you've redirected your nerves' firings and connections. Inevitably, any alteration in a given meaning will also shift every other subject matters' meanings that are linked to it.

For example, the word "piano" triggers a different meaning (and set of synapses) in someone who plays it on world stages than it does in a non-musician. Likewise, the meaning of "parent" activates different synapses in someone who has children than in one who doesn't. Meanwhile, if one day you find out that the people whom you saw as your biological parents turn out to be your adoptive ones, then the meaning of "parent" has shifted enormously, along with the associations that you've built up over the years.

The more meanings we are capable of conceiving, the more complex and vast our nervous system will, and must be. Neurological connections are the matrix from which we experience meaning, and without them no meaning can take place.[117] Concepts can dissolve when neurological connections disappear, which may be due to a new understanding, new information, maturity, and also from physical modifications. Please keep in mind that this neurological intricacy does not necessarily guarantee a logical relationship amongst the elements that add up to a meaning, as when a paranoid sees threats in innocent objects and events.

Two psychiatrists meet in a lobby. Dr Fern greets Dr Jennings and says: "I wish you a good morning." Dr Jennings thinks: "I wonder what he meant by that."

When we say that something gives our life meaning, it is because of how much of our neurology it engages. Anything at all can become meaningful if our nerves experience it that way. Just as different roads take us to vastly different places and situations, different neurological pathways cause us to perceive a range of meanings.[118]

For better or for worse, and like the cultivation of a fruit tree, clipping or fostering the branches of our neurological system can alter the meanings in our lives. This is possible because neurological relationships are not static, but fertile and evolving maps. Nerves can modify themselves, increase, compensate for damage, and respond to stimuli with a great degree of plasticity. They change due to our experiences as well as from our deliberate efforts to educate them.

We often use the word "meaning" when we are talking instead about a "sign". For example, when we say that increasing wind and looming dark grey clouds "mean" that it is going to rain soon, then we are making the word "mean" do the work of a sign. That wind and clouds are obvious signs of lurking rain is due to meteorological forces acting according to constant laws. The meaning of oncoming rain, however, differs for each person: "The coming rain means that I can't wear my suede shoes." "The coming rain means that I don't need to water my lawn."

None of these meanings is fixed. You might still wear those suede shoes if you get them waterproofed; perhaps you will still water the lawn because the rain was too sparse...and so on. Unlike the variables of meaning, the reliable signs of rain in the form of rising wind and grey clouds won't change, whether or not you wear your blue suede shoes, or if you water your lawn.

Most of the hard sciences are based upon this attitude of relying on objective signs rather than on meanings. Sciences tell us how things are constructed and how they work; they do not tell us what something means. That's why scientists can do research on stem cells and find it exciting work, while others think it "means" that they want to play God.

Conventional meanings bias our perceptions and cause us to act upon them automatically and without questioning their premises; this is the neurological source of stereotypes and prejudices. Unless we explore the validity of those meanings that we take for granted, we may be living a life of empty ones and never realize it. [119]

Stripping away all meaning is unnecessary in the ordinary

course of events. On the contrary, in its absence, we seek meaning as a way of saturating our feelings. When life becomes problematic, however, and precisely because of what something "means," then our ability to distinguish meanings from signs quickly helps reduce stressful neurological activity.

Meanings as Maps of Nerves

A simple and true-to-territory way to think of meanings is to see them as neurological maps with specific pathways: what I call: N-maps. As with physical ones, our neurological maps are where we have gone, can go, or will go. The fact that one neurological route became the more travelled does not remove the possibility that other paths to the same place could have been (and still can be) created.

As with external places, abandoning a well-worn trail results in it's becoming overgrown, whereas, repeatedly treading a new one eventually turns it into a familiar route. Changing one's N-maps comes from perceiving something in a different way and so, activating an alternative course of connecting synapses. N-maps also include places of meanings where we are trained not to go, or where we fear to go. These relate to taboo thoughts and actions, to subjects considered to be "bad", or deviant, and sometimes overt challenges to authority.

Don't even think of parking here!

Often, when we revisit past places and/or relationships, we find that we no longer can travel passageways to once accepted meanings. The opposite can also happen when past meanings flare up with as much fullness as if we had never been away. In this case, no decisive information formed a modified channel to create a revised meaning.

There are words and themes whose meanings for us throw a large shadow on other meanings because we associate them with degrees of self-worth and survivability. Words such as: love, success, race, failure, family, religion, health, and others. N-maps regarding any given subject are part of an active network whose neurological ends consist of both words and images. When we think of a given word, associated images conjure up its reality, and when we have a given image, multiple words get tagged to it.

Since the same word can be associated with different kinds of experiences, and just as a freeway exit branches out to different places, the paths of N-maps are segments of a network whose "word" locations connect with multiple roads.

Like all meanings, words require context for their intended content. The phrase "the knife is too dull" has completely different implications if we're cutting a sandwich rather than performing a surgery. Even though we understand that the "too dull" part is the point of the sentence, this dullness' application is the important aspect of its meaning. Each of the differing contexts has a neurological pathway to its distinct sense.

When we rethink a word or image and come to a fresh perception as to what they are "about", then, all our N-maps dependent upon that word's or image's participation are also redefined. The more critical either one's role, the more revolutionary the ripples of change throughout our neurological networks. Ideas simply on their own, are so powerful specifically because they can completely revise any number of N-maps in a single sweep, and through thought alone. As such, an idea's potentially uprooting power can cause people to resist it lest their neurons begin to respond to its possible materialization.

If we do not have the necessary nerve, then some imagined realities are too threatening to contemplate even in conceptual form. We might also have to alter our self-image just for having considered a controversial idea. This inflexibility protects the individual from any realizations that might cause them to adopt a—possibly, too radical—new way of being, along with its greater or lesser effects of re-routed neurology.

And because some words associated with a "forbidden" idea must nonetheless, also function elsewhere, such closed circuits can create damaging neighbourhoods of neurological resistance on matters that are not essentially controversial.

Daphne: You sold your sperm!
Martin: Stop using that word! Say "S"...
Niles: I sold my "S" to earn some money so I could buy Dad a Christmas present...
TV series, Frasier [120]

Any such stagnant N-maps render a person extremely rigid and unreasonable because they cannot process controversial activations between words that must also be used to speak about uncontroversial subjects. On the other hand, not having the nerve to contemplate something is a desirable trait when it comes to a latent potential for harm, or for the exploitation of others.

According to what is our attention's center stage, there is a greater or lesser neurological flow among all the N-maps. The flow of neurochemistry among our N-maps or else its absence, is the basis for either "feeling good" or "feeling bad". In the first case, uninterrupted transmission keeps the beat of the moment; there is minimal friction and all systems are "go". It is a day when we feel everything is going our way.

By contrast, when it's just not our day, then there are

bumper-to-bumper movements among N-maps as we stumble over uneven conceptual and emotional ground. A sense of flow can only arise when N-maps do not resist one another's transmissions or inhibitions. Turbulence usually arises when N-maps with more freedom are pitted against overly restraining ones, and vice versa.

An emerging set of published studies suggest that a brief self-affirmation activity at the beginning of a school term can boost academic grade-point averages in underperforming kids.[121]

The results of neuron-imaging offer solid proof that the words and images we use have decisive effects upon all of our physical and psychological systems. Mirror neurons especially, clearly illustrate the power of our imaginations over our bodies. As described also elsewhere, to view externally or to imagine internally, activates in us corresponding neurological pathways via mirror neurons. These cause us to respond as if we were acting with our own physicality what we are viewing or imagining. Just picture something that genuinely disgusts you and try to get into it. After only a brief time of doing this exercise, you might well want out.

This mirror-neuron process is what makes movies and spectator sports so popular. The catch though, is that the resultant desensitization of our nerves from their constant exposure to overly-sensationalized themes makes it ceaselessly necessary to pump up the texts and graphics. Movie scenes of violence and sex were once shown indirectly: waves crashing on rocks to represent physical passion; an arm sliding from an armchair to indicate a dead body.

Now, these themes are shown in high definition and graphic

detail so as to, literally, impress the jaded viewer's neurology into registering something new and so, remarkable. The fact is that: exposure to simulated violence has a stressful and downgrading effect on our nervous systems.[122]

This mirror neuronal process is, nonetheless, an invaluable aid for making desirable affirmations. Like blueprints for a new home, the constant imagining and planning of our desired state builds up neurological events into connected N-maps.[123]

Our body's health is directly impacted by the N-maps of our thoughts and feelings; it is our captive passenger during every neurological ride that we take. A poignant example is a person with multiple personalities. In an actual case, one "alter" has asthma and requires an inhaler to open the bronchioles of her lungs whenever she nears horses. However, another one of her alters does not, and can approach horses with no need whatsoever for medication. [124]

If a person's body can mimic symptoms of an illness to the point of requiring prescription medication, then it must be that affirmative self-concepts and visualizations act in the opposite direction and thus, trigger healed states and well-being.

On the lighter side, you have impersonators who can imitate a celebrity so vividly that they *are* that person. To a large degree, the impersonated person's way of being is indeed there because a good impersonator can adopt the N-maps of their subject. So much so that they can improvise as that character for a long time.

This capacity for behaving under the influence of a given personality's N-maps is the goal of any professional actor who willingly drops their private N-maps and substitutes those fitting to their role. It often happens that after playing romantic parts together, actors get so much into their latest role that they continue it off-screen (if only for a while).

The more technologically developed our culture is, the more our options in life are directly dependent on the range of meanings that we can understand, in how many languages, and the degree to which we can use them effectively with others. Based upon the customized meanings we give our words, we build a hall of mirrors from the projections that we lay onto others. How we think we are thought of, and how we think about others is framed by our assumptions of what N-maps must be active in them to be as they appear to us.

Whatever must you think of me?
Joan Crawford [125]

As we climb the socio-economic ladder, the neurological locations of things get more detailed and our vocabulary of words and their presumed meanings must expand accordingly. This is because, unfortunately, material success often leads to the practice of exclusion rather than inclusion. That's why there are books on etiquette; not because we haven't known for years how to eat fish with a fork, but in a more restricted social milieu we may not know the "proper" fork with which to eat it.

Using an N-map to reach for the "correct" utensil signals to others that not only can you maintain a smooth neurological flow in their medium, but also their own N-maps won't be disturbed by having to remove you from it.

35

KINDS OF MEANINGS

PART II

IN CONTRAST TO THE EASE WITH WHICH we can create meaning, it takes constant practice to remove it and see things as what they actually are: a neutral society of materials, whose meanings for each of us depend upon what we put center stage, and why. Meaning only arrives after somebody has tagged it to something that previously was meaningless. This association of words-to-things is exactly what becoming socialized and literate is all about.

However, unlike maps to external destinations, words are not located in quite the same place for everyone. Each of us can use the identical words and still be talking about very different realities. Consequently, hit-and-miss understandings occur all along the spectrum of human interactions.

On a global scale, this failure to communicate becomes inevitable when dissimilar cultural values and social roles lead to alternate experiences, and so to dissimilar N-maps for the meanings of words. Unfamiliar neurological relationships are compounded when we add such variables whereby a given object or situation might seem well known to us and yet, be strangely seen in other cultures.

Each of our unique N-maps give rise to divergent mentalities and worldviews, even when we think that we are using the same words, only translated. Confusion and conflicts readily surface when people expect one reaction from what they meant to say but instead get what the listener understood based upon their own N-maps about the supposedly same subject matter.

Due to cultural reflexes, that which is often considered obstinacy in another's position is merely the lack of somewhere else to go, neurologically speaking. The foreign nature of a concept and its applications may be so distant a neurological place that the other "can't get there from here". What we want them to feel and understand does not, and cannot, appear without a corresponding neurological territory to which they can go. Their neurological expansion can only come through additional information and thereby, new N-maps.

The royal road to genuine communication is not to expect conformity of usage, but to realize when a word's meaning differs for another. In that case, we can use interactive communication to affirm the intended message as compared with how else it is being heard. As communication is willingly re-combed until clarity has been mutually achieved, a true communion takes place. Those involved can tangibly feel a unity of consciousness, as if all had become one being regarding the topic at hand.

Knowing how to communicate is an education in both listening and in observing whether or not communication is actually taking place. It is as dependent upon these skills as it is upon our vocabulary.

CHILDISH N-MAPS

Some N-maps were formed so early in our lives that they create a chronic background rhythm of neurological expectation. For instance, repeated abuse from an early age on sets up an expectation that it will reappear whenever we find ourselves in situations that allow for this dynamic. Unfortunately, as in cases of a damaging childhood, we are attracted to similarly harmful situations because they feel like our first home.

Conversely, early N-maps that encode experiences of security and self-validation create a rich emotional account from which we can withdraw a sense of support whenever we need it.

Especially during childhood, the words that seep into us without our resistance have the result of seeds blown into a field: they take root and settle in. As we accept the way key words are used around us, their assumed meanings shape our perceptions and identities without challenge. By the time we enter adulthood, we often still live by the N-maps passed on to us since infancy.

These childhood N-maps are mostly based on our feelings and a limited access to nuanced vocabulary and reason. Associated with images and feelings rather than with words and ideas, the mental pictures that children compose are usually vague and sweeping in their conclusions and generalizations.

Rather than their thoughts, children's feelings are their primary guides for which way to go and for how to react. Whether they make logical sense or not, these pint-size points of view generally create the N-maps that will underlie and support their future adult ones.

Unless there is a compelling enough motivation to do so, there will rarely be a root-directory reconfiguration of this infantile worldview. This is why we can lose our adult sense of autonomy when we revisit the places and people of our early life. We then obviously come under the spells of our precognitive experiences and of their first unquestioned N-maps.

SOCIAL N-MAPS

The verbal dependency of Western societies results in countless N-maps that center on keywords: justice, freedom, opportunity, fairness, peace, love, equality, truth, rights, and others. In supposed service of these words, the triad of Religion, Science, and Art each have their chance to infiltrate its own targeted N-maps into us.

Since they have no detached external product, religions use ritualized words to create N-maps that promote preferred behaviour in their followers. From another approach, science's need for proof has the constant potential to remove existing N-maps, in parallel with installing new ones.

Meanwhile, Art offers us the conditions to anarchically try on alternative ways of perceiving realities, and to do so with minimal social consequences—except when the art product touches a social nerve.

Whereas, religion and science come with clear implications of representing "real" reality as the basis for their authority, art objects and events come without any such obligation to take them seriously—hence the great freedom art offers both to artists and to their audiences.

Paradoxically, the N-maps fostered by the arts are some of the most influential and revolutionary in the long run, precisely because they don't start with an N-map that could trigger resistance by overtly stating its aspect of "real" reality. The power of Art should not come as a surprise, however, because it is all about creation—an activity identical to life's own.

N-MAPS OF OBJECTS

Buyers expand their self-concepts to include a given object's N-maps of meanings, whose egos they then add to their own. The entire build-up of a brand name is precisely to create desirable associations of meanings and feelings with products. This strategy notwithstanding, increasingly there are N-maps of conscientiousness about the manufacturing process itself and its effects on the sustainability and wellbeing of global resources. A social consciousness will inevitably create new neurological pathways and refashion N-maps of purchasing behaviour.

Vintage/historical objects come with their own flavour of enfolded N-maps that automatically stimulate our imaginations. We can extend feelings into any antique/historical object by conceptualizing its time, owner, and role. We imagine what it must have been like when... or who once interacted with an object, and why. In the process, our existing N-maps expand since we now have the right to describe how close we've come to a given object and its pedigree it becomes associated with our own. The background stories of historical or rare objects further demand N-maps as to what constitutes an authority and an expert.

N-maps of Addiction

Whenever we use an addictive substance, we open the door for it to create N-maps whose neurological circuits allow it to have its way with us. By letting it in to begin with, we have dropped our firewall against unchecked chemical forces and so risk being at the mercy of our weakest neurological links.

Although we may first reach for drugs based upon an N-map of curiosity or peer pressure, continuous use lets the addictive substance hijack our neurology and begin its mathematics of our needing ever more of it.

Only when we can connect with the N-map of a self-concept with greater gravitational pull than that of the addicting substance will we be able to transform ourselves–sometimes very quickly–into a state of liberation and autonomy. The twist is to persevere in finding that self-concept, which always exists latent within us.

Miscellaneous N-maps

The essence of neuroticism is a disproportionately active series of N-maps whose effects on our thoughts, feelings, and actions, overshadow their intended function of accurately informing our perceptions. Instead, they overwhelm us with their own looped activities, as is the case with compulsive behaviours.

Beginner's luck has an N-map that tends to disappear after the initial experience. As they repeat the activity, the spontaneous skill often shown by beginners, is lost. That's because their first attempts had the N-map of "I've never done this before, so if I fail, it doesn't really mean anything." The beginner is thus relaxed and lets the thing, in great part, do itself—which is exactly the ultimate skill that masters cultivate.

After that, the N-maps of "can I do it as well this time?" or "what if I fail..." and other thoughts of that nature seep in. The beginner's initial self-forgetfulness has dissolved into newly triggered scenarios, and these are going to skew any physical skills in the direction of self-consciousness and away from the flow of letting the actions do themselves.

Winning & losing each have a specific kind of N-map that leads to those self-images reinforced and broadcast by a society's media. Generally, winners are applauded and losers...not so much. The brutality of this simplistic categorization is behind educational movements that seek to eliminate competitive activities and in this way, neutralize the polar emotional charges that are now attached to these two words.

Certain professions require the absence of N-maps in order to be optimally performed. Doctors cannot have N-maps of revulsion in front of blood and other bodily elements. Police officers must not obviously identify with those whom they imprison. Military personnel cannot afford to have too many N-maps of empathy but rather, require those of obedience and strategy. The purpose of boot camp is in fact, to remove the recruits' N-maps of sensitivity, non-conformity, and self-direction.

N-maps of authority intend to assure neurological congruence among those who believe in it. However, when there is no trust in the authority, then social coherence falls apart as each individual directs themselves according to the N-maps of their own self-determination and interests.

A desire for relief from certain N-maps and the activation of simpler ones, as when we go away on vacation. Closer to home, meditation offers the willful suspension and quieting of N-maps as a way of giving our various physical and psychological systems a rest. Through such displacements as these, we feel relief because we no longer bear the meaning-masses of our usual neurological activities.

Commonality and agreement lead to congruence between people's N-maps. The resonance of similar N-maps is very soothing and can go very deep. Any large group or organization is itself a merger of N-maps. It's capacity to function is based on how much its member's nervous systems are in support of the group's cause.

The N-maps of initial social meetings are usually favourable because of insufficient information for mistrust to appear. With increasing details come specific issues of neurological fit between individuals or groups. This naturally leads to either more expansion, or else, to more contraction between individuals.

There is no end to how many N-maps can be formed, and that is the key point. Human life cannot be separated from both the formation, and the experiencing of N-maps. It's up to each of us to cultivate the ones that we wish to experience.

36

TRUTH

Kaffee: "I want the truth!"
Col. Jessep: " You can't handle the truth! [126]

TO KNOW THE TRUTH IS TO KNOW the whole story, all the parts, their relationships, and what motivated their movements down to the slightest intentions and forces of all beings involved. This complete recall and access to information is generally out of reach because there are too many elements to include.

A truth is sometimes easy to process because it involves a clear action: "The eggs fell." The "what happened" of even such a simple event, however, can depend upon the honesty of the primary actor: "I sneezed." "You startled me." "The eggs began to jiggle."

Truth is not something that is a part of anything but instead, the human evaluation of a subject matter's authenticity. Any unchanging truth about something requires total information along with our neurological capacity to process it. Once we accredit something as a "truth", we must inevitably manage its impact upon us. Since it is viewed as "the end of the line" and gives us no greater reality to go to, an unpleasant truth can feel very ruthless once revealed.

The consequence flowing from truth's dependence upon both information and its incorporation into perception is that:

although we can agree on truths noticeable to all (rain falls from the sky), we cannot always agree on truths that originate from inner processes transmitted as information.

As a variation on the theme of truth, if we are unable to perceive something's existence then we cannot assert its truth, even if there is the potential for verification under other circumstances. Some birds see beyond the spectrum of visible light and perceive the ultraviolet wavelengths of flowers. If, in ignorance of this fact, we insist that no such floral wavelength exists, are we lying or telling the truth? Where lies the truth when we all agree on a lie based upon misinformation?

Because some people's nervous system has an above average sensitivity, they may be aware of a truth even as others firmly deny its existence. Along the same lines, a person may perceive something accessible only to them, such as hallucinations, or perhaps other dimensions of life. In either case, the truth remains elusive for the group and actual for the individual.

Unlike other variables such as length, width, mass, or time of day, colour is not an inherent property of the object; it is a property of the nervous system of the animal perceiving the light.[127]

There are many global conditions that are of concern to us as empathetic beings: hunger, wars, sustainability, and sad to say, much more. We have differing "truths" on these subject matters because we are acting out of unique personal nervous systems.

Some truths can be measured by a simple "yes" or "no" because they are clearly absolute states of being. Is a person pregnant or not? Or how about: is there a ghost in the room? This last question cannot always be answered in a clear way.

The neurology of some people registers the presence of a being whom others do not see, like children with their imaginary friends.

How can a person who does not perceive that someone else is in the room agree that the other who does see them is telling the truth? The fact is that the truths of inner realities are well beyond the reach of external measurements and can only be shared when another person says: "me too."

Thoughts, feelings, imaginations, all fill our ungraspable inner world, the specifics of which must always be reenacted, and privately so. An object in mind must be newly imagined every time that we think of it; there is no inner shelf to which we can return in the expectation of finding a previous thought still there. We cannot take a photograph of our inner space and show its contents to someone else. All that we can do is to express it, or act under its influence.

Is it the truth that reality is malleable to the extent of being transformable by anyone and at will? Since truth is based upon neurological activity, the answer to this question emerges from personal experience. Whether all or a few say that it is true, the truth of a self-determined reality can only reveal itself within each of our own lives.

Truth is the daughter of time, not of authority.
Francis Bacon, Philosopher, 1561–1626

The point of being able to transform reality is relevant to our own personal experience. As long as we achieve our desired results, it makes no practical difference if others believe that a flexible reality is true or not.

37

SPACE-CHANGE CONTINUUM

People like us, who believe in physics, know that the distinction between past, present, and future is only a stubbornly persistent illusion. Albert Einstein

OUR CONCEPTS OF REALITY ARE SEEDS whose blueprints determine what will grow into our experiences. As with the physical kind, a conceptual seed's built-in activation sets off a chain of tangible events, whereby each stage's dynamics give rise to the next one, right on up to the seed's finalized being.

With physical seeds, we get obvious proof of their viability since we can plant them and see if anything grows. So it is with a conceptual seed. If the concept that we can each transform our reality is accurate then we can and should expect proofs that will justify our investment in it. What usually undercuts our results are pre-existing, conflicting concepts about reality's inflexible structures and doubts as to our merits.

One of these undermining beliefs is the linearity of time, whereby events must occur one after the other and in the right order: to get from 2 to 5, you seemingly have no choice but to first go through 3 and 4. Although an impression of irreversible movement towards "the future" is indeed necessary for us to experience reality as we usually do, it is not essential to live along a fixed horizontal track of time, as trains must. In fact, we already don't.

Each of our linear movements forward is merged with non-sequential time travels within us. We might be riding from one place to another, but during that space, we've also travelled inwardly to our vacation last summer, our evening destination, our childhood, the groceries we must get tomorrow, etc. Just as we hyperlink inwardly with our thoughts, so we can catalyze the changes that we want to appear outwardly. To initiate this skill, we first need to view each step forward in terms of change, not of time.

The "space-time continuum" is a conventional expression to describe how each of the subjects, space and time are intertwined. This model gives time equal status with that of space. I disagree, for whereas space is fundamental—nothing would have a place for itself without it—regular time is not. What time was it before clocks were made? The changes that any time measures must pre-exist before they can be "timed."

Life happens through the phenomenon of changes in the contents of space, which makes change the official partner of space, not time. Like a globe's designed grid of longitudes and latitudes, time is only layered over changes within space. Time is simply the uniform that we force change to wear. Locking changes into equally divided spaces of units did not appear until someone fulfilled the concept of clocks. Being "on time" emerged from the desire of certain humans to plan meetings: people with events, people with machines, people with people.[128]

Thanks to timepieces, we can locate ourselves in the exact same space, at the same moment as something else, like a train—regardless of what we had to do to assure that we arrived "on time". [129] Because Western cultures routinely train us to see time as a fixed reality, we are generally unaware that not all cultures experience time, nor if they do, that they experience it another way. [130]

No one is born with the innate ability to recognize numerals.[131]

Meanwhile, whereas each change is unique in its way, time must fit itself to the scale of what is being measured, from light-years for stars, to nanoseconds for subatomic events. The common factor among them is that time's differences occur in equalized intervals between fixed points. This evenness makes of time a monotone; it has beats, but no rhythm.

By contrast, unmeasured change has a rhythm that always reflects the nature of the changing thing, and not necessarily meted out in equal units. The various alterations of life announce seasonal modifications that come from inner prompts, which are themselves activated by variables such as temperature and light.

Biological clocks have growth spurts, dormant periods, and work within vast tolerances. They also adapt to altered circumstances and can undergo changes at different rates than before; what used to appear at one point now comes either earlier or later, or never. Just as with plants and animals, this organic rhythm is better suited to people than are the equal ticks of an industrial clock.

We would be far more in touch with life's movements if we thought in terms of a space-change continuum rather than one of time partnered with space. The concept that transformations, great and small, occur from change rather than from time lets us be at ease with the idea of space's contents as independent from the rigidly linear process called "cause and effect."

It is far easier to accept a malleable reality when we perceive time as an artificial network and instead, focus ourselves on sensing change with all its variable points and underlying pulses. To be able to think of a change in our circumstances in this way frees us from measuring how much time *must* pass before a change is likely to appear—and from speculating in what way the sequence of changes will come about. Otherwise, looking at how much time a change is taking, and through what means, is a stumbling block towards letting a change take place in its own way, and at its own pace.

By thinking in terms of change rather than time, we are untangled from any expectations as to what specific parts need to appear, and in what order. Instead, we can place our attention and feelings on the emerging changed state itself. This focus sensitizes us to internal prompts for action and to recognizing goal-specific opportunities as they appear—which they will. Once we see change as a fundamental and holistic unit, then we can easily understand the potential for situations to be transformed according to the activated energies of our imaginations and feelings.

The more we pay attention to our inner world's contents and observe their echo in our outer world, the faster materializations from imagination to outer reality seem to go. They increasingly appear to dispense with linear, consecutive cause and effect, and to work mostly through pure change instead, as if from out of the blue. Whereas time requires a development from minute to minute, from day to day, change can come immediately and from anywhere.

When we invest in imagining our reality as we wish it to be, its alteration will happen through a process of morphing, form's least resisting dynamic for change. It consists of a smooth and much-condensed mutation of one thing into something else that is significantly other. Many of us have seen movies that show the morphing of the appearance of one person into another. As we visually and conceptually follow the changes, the reasons to their transformations seem to respect a kind of logical sense.

As long as there is a superficial connection between a reality's "before" and "after," and as long as any transformation is in the direction of our needs and desires, then we won't scrutinize the logic of new opportunities, new situations, or sudden inputs of information. Quite the contrary, we will have been primed for such change by our ongoing imagination of how it would be, and how it would feel if a longed-for reality did appear. Our feelings and imagination will have repeatedly tried it on for size and so there will be an element of familiarity to its arrival, even amid its suddenness.

However surprising, this change of reality will nonetheless seem to be based on its own logic—a necessary aspect for our psychological balance and sense of reality's homeostasis. Without the latter, we feel insecure as to whether any change has really come, and when it has, if it can last.

That said, since we rarely ever conduct an extensive retrospective analysis, we have no documentable way of knowing how logical a change in our life circumstances is. More than that, our brains organize all new information such that we could have a completely nonsensical logic, and we would still accept it as true. This is as it should be because it is more important for a desired change to occur than it is to be able to prove that it did so in regular and rational increments.

Life is not about logic, but about creativity and vitality, which always have their own self-contained reasoning. In addition, if searched for, there will always be an explanation, one based on new information as to why a given change appeared, sometimes including an irresistible tug to be where a serendipitous encounter/opportunity took place.

The changes in our life all end up as the unfolded text of our own story and as with a novel, there is no need to spell out every different element between one chapter and the next. The fact is that no one can write the complete story of even their own life. Instead, we recall our past in the same way that a movie is constructed; in scenes and dialogues.

Logic will always play an important part; just as mechanical clocks are useful tools that secure our actions. As it is, most of life's aesthetics and music depend upon a retraceable stream of events set in motion at a certain point and played out at another. This kind of sequencing is the track upon which any storyline travels. Without some such degree of unfolding, everything would be happening at once, and in a nonsensical way.

A seemingly logical development is essential for human experience to specifically be as it is: the build-up of events, predictable growth, seasonal changes, plots and their finale, birth to death, genetic development, discoveries, history, musical composition, investments, infinity. These are the plays of life that we all get to influence and to participate in.

The more insight we have into the nature of creativity and its processes, the more we can appreciate how the linearity of, so-called "every day" is a technical aspect that is essential for our unique human experiences. Endless human contexts and products depend upon its seemingly absolute character. However, we are misdirected—as with a magic act—when we make linear time the controlling concept for our options to influence the contents of our lives.

Transforming our reality is possible via collaboration between the crossfield of being and ourselves. Its orchestration of information and influences from a multitude of sources provides us with the wanted changes. They appear in the form of new opportunities and new information whose potential we still need to act upon to fullfill.

The transformation of reality is not about things falling out of the air, but about things arriving and falling into place.

38

Breathing 101

Many spiritual disciplines emphasize the importance of deep and deliberate breathing, and with good reason. With the space that it introduces, breathing literally expands our capacity to receive and process deeper layers of sensual information. Churches intuitively know this, which is why most of them have very high ceilings and large rooms.

With its introduction of space, breathing moves organic, emotional, intellectual, and psychological elements away from each other. Consequently, the circulation of all systems–from cells, to liquids, to feelings, to thoughts, to actions–can now flow uncompressed into their optimal relationships in relation to one another. As forced contact among these parts is reduced, the demands on our neurological systems also diminish and we begin to expand within.

The practice of deliberate breathing, especially in combination with meditation, strengthens and stabilizes our nervous system. It also creates an opportunity to feel comfortable amid emptiness. Just as there are infinite subject matters possible on a blank canvas, in the void of space everything's materialization is latent as pure potential.

Conscious breathing catalyzes a dynamic that draws out what inspires and motivates us. By applying our inspirations to a desired content, we can extract a transformed reality from the space offered by our breaths.

A simple companion practice to conscious breathing is that of regular meditation. Meditation develops our stance into that of a detached observer who has neither interacting or reacting. It gives our consciousness a retreat from the work of managing our lives' texts and textures. This practice—without the need for any accompanying belief system—strengthens our capacity to get off the stage and to just be the spectator of whatever comes before us. In this way, we return to our source state as pure consciousness. Meditation stretches our inner space, which eventually gives us greater perspective to sense the bigger picture and what actions and behaviours will benefit us in the long run.

Without such expanding tools as breathing and meditation, we often do not have the luxury of a space from which to contemplate how a given reality is constructed or where it is likely to go. Consequently, we are pulled into events without a viewpoint from which to challenge their ruling concepts. We then assume that something is either inevitable or else necessary, which then leads us to act reflexively instead of reflectively.

Notwithstanding the above, when things are going well we do not want to dispel our experiences by adding too much space into our lives. Instead, we seek to be ever more saturated with our present reality and do not want it to be diluted. This intensity of being is part of any vital functionality. Only our full absorption of life can provide complete information at each moment to the crossfield and so optimize its role as a benevolent collaborator.

However, when we come under pressure or distress, then we want to dispel certain aspects of our reality. To do so, we must be able to increase our inner space and look at how the situation is constructed from a conceptual point of view. In all cases, our feelings and thoughts will arise from the activation of N-maps triggered by the words and images we use to describe our situation.

The description may be concrete (I'm sick, poor, happy, lucky), but the heart and spirit of this representation is how a given situation echoes what we currently feel and think about ourselves, and in combination with what we think reality allows.

Who do you think you are that you belong within a certain situation, and why do you feel that you deserve to be in it? The answers constitute the forces by which you are bound to your own story. Change your answer and you must also change the dynamics by which you think you're "forced" to live.

Here is where deliberate breathing calms us enough to be able to step back and observe our problematic situation's ruling dynamics. New insights, thoughts and feelings can then arise out of the space we've just created; with them come a fresh sense of enlightenment and a reduction in the situation's mass.

Due to our expanded viewpoint and the information that it brings, we can now disperse our former conviction that the problem is solid and absolute. Instead, we see it as something that we have densified with our thoughts and feelings, but can now dissolve by using our desire-directed will to start drawing-out the changes that we want.

As soon as this potential is reclaimed, a part of us naturally dissolves into the crossfield (Source, if you prefer), from which new information then arises to direct us into a solution. Our self-examinations will continue to reveal what concepts of power and disempowerment must be involved for the current situation to have its problematic character. We do not need to figure out how the moment's repair will come into being or what it will be. We need only change the emotional tone of our perceptions by imagining a rerouting of the situation towards the better. From then on, the problem stops being fed and its dissolution is underway.

This approach is not the latest set of rose-coloured glasses, but a call for life's limitless creativity to reconfigure information and then create something beneficial with the elements at play. It can always do so, and when called upon it always does because the essence of any being is raw creation directed with ingenuity. Similarly to a new drawing in a sketchbook, every moment in life can be a turned page upon which we draw out new content.

If we can springboard ourselves to such a view, then the crossfield will fluidly organize a restoration of wellbeing, and even deliver a bonus through the repair of related complications. This self-healing process is part of the creative tide that ebbs and flows between our individual autonomy and our universal home base.

As we work our way from the macro level to the micro vibratory source of all being, we realize that our thoughts and feelings are filled with spaces from which we can exit a problem and in a holistic way, enter its solution. Inevitably, this viewpoint guides us towards a restoration of our wellbeing within a new set of circumstances in which we are sufficiently relaxed to give a sigh of relief and so, naturally breathe deep.

39

RELAX, IT'S ONLY ALIGNMENT

IF YOU CAN VISUALIZE THE INTERSECTING angles of an x-y-z graph, with each axis perfectly extended along its perpendicular, then you will clearly see a representation of true relaxation combined with alertness.

This 3D graph's zero meeting point is where we cannot help but feel relaxed because we are now neurologically aligned vis à vis the various directions in which life's forces can travel. The essence of relaxation, and of self-confidence is to maintain this alignment regardless of the forces acting upon us.

One technique towards re-orienting ourselves in this way is to visualize the current status of our inner x-y-z axes according to how we are feeling at any given moment. Whenever we are out of sorts, anxious, afraid, insecure, etc., we can clearly visualize and sense how our lack of self-composure is reflected in the axes' off-kilter relationships. The solution is, using our imagination, to restore the lines to the perpendicular and so regain natural balance.

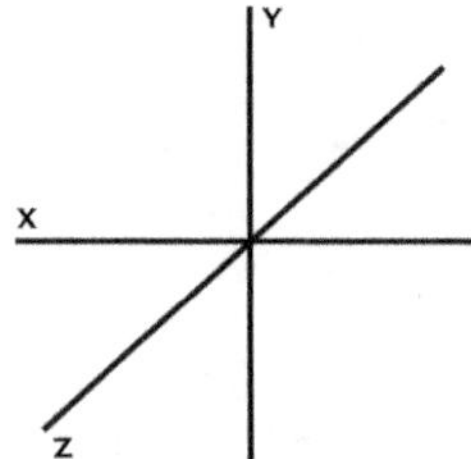

40

All Clear

> *And highlighted the next step as a shift to "radical transparency" where the "whole product development process [is] laid bare, and opened to customer input."*
> 132

What is clear provides transparency such that space and light can go through it; things other than itself then become the focus of attention.

There are a handful of naturally clear human states that are invisible and silent when pure, but obstacles to well-being when they are not.

1. *Air is clear;* it nourishes us with its oxygen and poisons us when it is no longer transparent.

2. *Light is clear* and invisible; it only appears when reflected to us as that which it illuminates. The light itself remains indifferent as to what it reveals.

3. *Consciousness is clear* unless its natural follow-through is ignored. When we act against it, our inner world creates noise where there once was peaceful silence.

4. *Health is clear* and weightless when present. There are an infinite number of unhealthy states, but the degrees of deviation away from a healthy one are few.

5. *Freedom is clear,* and we can move through it without hindrance.

6. *Flow is clear* of friction; it is the desired rhythm for all motion.

7. *To think clearly* is to not use incomplete information to come to a complete conclusion.

8. *To see clearly* is to see what presents itself, combined with what cannot be seen, or seeks to hide.

9. *To see clearly* is to not see what isn't there,

10. *To hear clearly* is not to hear what wasn't said.

11. *To hear clearly* is to hear what is being expressed, along with what remains unspoken.

12. *To act clearly* is not necessarily to know the full outcome of our actions, but to recognize that the time to be still has ended.

13. *Ethics are clear;* they enable the right way to manifest itself such that we do not have cause in the future to regret the decisions and actions of the past.

41

Nao

The paradigm of the organic self is not intended to be yet another belief system, but a structural way of thinking about our lives and then exercising a complete range of options by leveraging reality's malleability.

Nonetheless, the linear nature of literacy and information forces us as with any subject matter, to give it an identity. By doing so we create a nucleus around which associated information can gather and upon which we can focus our attention.

The *organic self* is no exception to this requirement, and its identity is what I call "Nao", a combination of the individualistic and freeform Western concept of the "Now" and the adaptive cooperative Eastern philosophy of the "Tao".

Now + Tao = Nao.

End-Notes

1 / p. 9: Please see chapter 27: The Mention of Dimensions; page 146.

2 / p. 11: Please see chapter 19: Nothing Really Matters; page 112.

3 / p. 11: http://www.livescience.com/8869-8-shocking-learned-stephen-hawking-book.html.

4 / p. 11: "Quantum" is Latin for "quantity."; "quidquid" is Latin for "whatever".

5 / p. 13: Brian Witte, Military grooms new officers for war in cyberspace. April 26, 2013, The Associated Press

6 / p. 15: "Can A Jellyfish Unlock the Secret of Immortality." By Nathaniel Rich; http://www.nytimes.com/2012/12/02/magazine/can-a-jellyfish-unlock-the-secret-of-immortality.html?pagewanted=1&_r=0&ref=general&src=me

7 / p. 16: Please see chapter 7: Hand Over Your Heart; p. 37

8 / p. 17: Please see chapter 25: W/Inner; page 136.

9 / p. 17: Jacob Jolij and Maaike Meurs of the Psychology Department of the U. of Groningen. www.sciencedaily.com/releases/2011/04/110427101606.htm.

10 / p. 19: Mirror neurons are the neurological firings that mirrors what one is looking such that it creates a simulation in the perceiver that is in keeping with the witnessed action.

11 / p. 19: Please see chapter 33: Word's Worth; page 171.

12 / p.21: Please see chapter 27: The Mention of Dimensions, and chapter 20: Now is a Stem Cell: pages 146 and 118.

13 / p. 22: *Eugen Herrigel - Zen in the Art of Archery*

14 / p.24: Please see chapter 22, In the Spirit of Things, page 124.

15 / p. 27: The lucid dream state can be developed into a frequent event through exercises. Although it has been publicized only since the last half of the twentieth century, lucid dreaming has been referenced in different ages and places, including in the Far East as a form of yoga; Dream Yoga.

16 / p. 31: "On Wednesday, Tarleton was able to turn her head and embrace Marinda Righter, the daughter of her tissue donor. Righter, who had first met Tarleton the day before, called their meeting a 'magical' experience. –abcnews.go.com/Health/woman-disfigured-lye-attack-reveals-face/story?id=19082675

17 / p. 32: "Emmy was the ship's cat on the RMS Empress of Ireland. She was an orange tabby cat who never missed a voyage. However, on May 28, 1914, Emmy tried to escape the ship. The crew could not coax her aboard and the Empress left without her. She was reportedly last seen on the roof of the shed at Pier 27, watching her ship sail out of Quebec City. Early the next morning the Empress collided with the SS Storstad while steaming through fog at the mouth of the St. Lawrence river and rapidly sank, killing over 1,000 people." –en.wikipedia.org/wiki/Ship's_cat

18 / p. 33: http://www.newscientist.com/article/mg21128285.900-quantuN-minds-why-we-think-like-quarks.html?full=true&print=true

19 / p. 34: Unlike light, however, consciousness can illuminate forms within our inner world as well as our outer one.

20 / p. 35: surethingsugar–www.buzzfeed.com/mattbellassai/the-creepiest-things-a-child-has-ever-said-to-a-parent. For more information on the subject, there's the deeply researched book: Children Who Remember Previous Lives: A Question of Reincarnation; by Ian Stevenson. 2000 edition

21 / p. 37: The etymology of "discourage" is literally "away from the heart": "discourage (v.) mid-15c., discoragen, from Middle French descourager, from Old French descoragier, from des- "away" (See: dis) + corage (See: courage)." "courage (n.) c.1300, from Old French corage (12c., Modern French courage) "heart, innermost feelings; temper," from Vulgar Latin *coraticum (source of Italian coraggio, Spanish coraje), from Latin cor "heart" (See: heart) which remains a common metaphor for inner strength." ©: www.etymonline.com Douglas Harper, Feb. 28, 2013.

22 / p. 41: Please see chapter 13: Love...Tell Me More; page 73.

23 / p. 42: http://en.wikipedia.org/wiki/Feral_child

24 / p. 43: "These service interactions are a performance, much like a theatrical one where each party has its roles to play," the authors write. "But the scripts are not neutral; rather, they reflect the customers' desire to reenact their class-based dominance over their hairdressers." However, service workers are not powerless in these situations:
"On the contrary, the game that is being played is what we call an interdependent status game, where customers are as much dependent on the service providers as service providers are on customers," the authors conclude.
Tuba Üstüner and Craig J. Thompson. How Marketplace Performances Produce Interdependent Status Games and Contested Forms of Symbolic Capital. Journal of Consumer Research, February 2012.

25 / p. 43: Former model going to school in "Picture Me," a movie of her life

26 / p. 43: Just google your name. In some parts of the middle east, women are not given a name at all but identified by their relationship to family members: So-and-so's daughter.. .wife....sister....

27 / p. 44: Park notes that women, in particular, are socialized from a young age to be romantically desirable..."
"'Gender scripts discourage women from appearing intelligent in masculine domains, like STEM,'" Park says, "and in fact, studies show that women who deviate from traditional gender norms, such as succeeding in male-typed jobs, experience backlash for violating societal expectations." [Science, technology, engineering and math (STEM.)] – L. E. Park, A. F. Young, J. D. Troisi, R. T. Pinkus. Effects of Everyday Romantic Goal Pursuit on Women's Attitudes Toward Math and Science. Personality and Social Psychology Bulletin, 2011; 37 (9).

28 / p. 48: Charles Fernyhough, The voices within: The power of talking to yourself. New Scientist, 03 June 2013.

29 / p. 49: Pensive: "...mid-14c., from O.Fr. pensif (11c., fem. pensive), from penser "to think," from L. pensare "weigh, consider," frequentative of pendere "weigh" (See: pendant)."
Expense: "...late 14c., from Anglo-Fr. expense, O.Fr. espense "money provided for expenses," from L.L. expensa "disbursement, outlay, expense," prop. neut. pl. pp. of L. expendere "to weigh out money, to pay down" (See: expend)."
Expend: "...early 15c., from L. expendere "pay out, weigh out

money," from ex- "out" (See: ex) + pendere "to pay, weigh" (See: pendant). Related: Expended; expending." – http://www.etymonline.com/ (2010.) All etymologies thanks to © Douglas Harper.

30 / p. 49: Please see chapter 28: Mass Appeal; page 148.

31 / p. 49: Serious: "...mid-15c., "expressing earnest purpose or thought" (of persons), from M.Fr. sérieux "grave, earnest" (14c.), from L.L. seriosus, from L. serius "weighty, important, grave.."
– http://www.etymonline.com/ (2010) © Douglas Harper

32 / p. 50: www.newscientist.com/article/mg21428611.100-poor-little-rich-minds-the-price-of-wealth.html?full=true

33 / p. 51: Please see chapter 4: The Crossfield of Being; p. 22.

34 / p. 53: Dealbook.nytimes.com/2012/04/04/living-like-a-billionaire-if-only-for-a-day/?hp

35 / p. 55: www.nytimes.com/2012/02/26/arts/design/authenticity-of-trove-of-pollocks-and-rothkos-goes-to-court.html?_r=1&hp

36 / p. 57: "In fact, some people avoid ill-gotten gains – such as from unfair labor practices or insider trading – for fear of 'moral contagion,'... "Though we often think $50 is $50, these results demonstrate that when money takes on negative moral associations, its value is diminished." – University of California - Berkeley (2013, April 23). People care about source of money, attach less value to 'tainted' wealth. – ScienceDaily. Retrieved April 25, 2013, from http://www.sciencedaily.com¬/releases/

37 / p. 60: An Unloved Masterpiece
"Sometimes you just don't like a painting, no matter how 'great' it is. That's how one Scottish woman felt in the early 1960s, when her husband came home with a painting of roses that she disliked enough to banish to a spare room... The BBC reports that the painting in question was recently identified as Pink Roses, an original oil work by one of Scotland's most influential artists, Samuel Peploe, valued by McTear's Auctioneers in Glasgow at £300,000. "
www.huffingtonpost.com/2013/01/14/diego-rivera-found-office-door-antiques-road-show_n_2471089.html#slide=1931398

38 / p. 62: Please see chapters 12, and 23: Consciousness as Sensual Information, and Real Good: pages 66, and 128

39 / p. 62: By Gene Weingarten; April 11, 2013. www.washingtonpost.com/opinions/a-story-that-makes-roger-ebert-look-bad-too-soon/2013/04/11/0b622ae8-a21c-11e2-9c03-6952ff305f35_story.html?hpid=z2

40A / p. 64: "The Mexicans have invested billions in greenhouses to grow tomatoes, while Florida tomatoes are largely picked green and treated with a gas to change their color." – www.nytimes.com/2013/02/04/business/united-states-and-mexico-reach-deal-on-tomato-imports.html?_r=0

40-B / p. 64: Kate Connolly; "I wish I'd made a lawnmower"; The Guardian. July 29, 2002.

41 / p. 66: Please see chapter 26: Form, the Universal Factor

42 / p. 69: Alexander Pope, Essay on Criticism, 1709.

43 / p. 70: www.bradenton.com/2013/04/12/4479351/mother-of-toddler-injured-in-lawn.html

44 / p. 73: Bertrand Russel; 1872–1970. Nobel laureate in Literature, mathematician, philosopher, historian, political activist.

45 / p. 75: Brian Switek, My Beloved Brontosaurus... By Farrar, Straus and Giroux.

46 / p. 78: Written by user name "GTRich2004." http://www.mensdivorcelawblog.com/2012/when-did-you-realize-it-was-over/

47 / p. 79: "As Colt observed of his siblings, and it's true of mine as well, they aren't people he would have likely made an effort to know or spend time with if he'd met them at school, say, or at work. And yet a reunion with them thrills him more than a reunion with friends, who don't make him feel that he's "a part of a larger quilt," he said. His brothers do." www.nytimes.com/2013/05/26/opinion/sunday/bruni-the-gift-of-siblings.html pagewanted=2&ref=general&src=me – The Gift of Siblings, by Frank Bruni, May 25, 2013

48 / p. 79: www.slate.com/articles/life/dear_prudence/2013/04/dear_prudence_my_sister_in_law_tried_to_seduce_me.html

49 / p. 79: Please see chapter 28: Mass Appeal; page 148.

50 / p. 82: Bachelorette Ashley, Season 7, talking about her experience of fixing up an orphanage in Thailand.

51 / p. 83: Since working on the project, MacKinnon has been able to bring her own sleep paralysis episodes under control – or at least learned to calm herself during them. The trick, she said, is to use episodes like a form of research, by paying attention to details like how her hands feel and what position she's in. This sort of mindfulness tends to make scary hallucinations blink away, she said."
www.livescience.com/28325-spooky-filN-explores-sleep-paralysis.html

52 / p. 85: -www.belfasttelegraph.co.uk/news/world-news/gunman-kill-six-in-russian-town-of-belgorod-because-someone-had-scratched-his-car-29214494.html. By Shaun Walker - 23 April 2013

53 / p. 86: Stanford School of Engineering (2011, October 14). Engineers create touchscreen Braille writer.

54 / p. 92: Please see chapter 23: Real Good; page 128.

55 / p. 92: Please see chapter 11: Egos Everywhere I Go; page 58.

56 / p. 93: Please see chapter 22: In the Spirit of Things; page 124.

57 / p. 93: Please see chapters 34 and 35: Kinds of Meanings, Parts I & II; pages 178, and 188.

58 / p. 94: Please see chapter 24; Prove My Faith; p. 131.

59 / p. 96: http://tech.fortune.cnn.com/2011/10/06/steve-jobs-the-best-of-the-obits/ – Steve Jobs: The best of the obits – By Phillip Elmer-DeWitt, October 6, 2011

60 / p. 105: www.huffingtonpost.com/2014/06/23/divorce-reasons-n-5522650.html - The Moment I Knew, slideshow.

61 / p. 106: Apotemnophilia

62 / p. 106: Capgras Delusion

63 / p. 106: Cotard's Syndrome

64 / p. 106: Congenital insensitivity to pain (CIPA); Prosopagnosia.

65 / p. 107: At the rare book section of the former Anthroposophic Center on Madison Avenue and 35th street..

66 / p. 107: Wikipedia: Monopod

67 / p. 108: "Leudar and Thomas (2000) inVoices of Reason, Voices of Insanity, review almost 3,000 years of voice-hearing history, including that of Socrates, Schreber, and Janet's patient 'Marcelle,' amongst others, to show how we have moved the experience from a socially valued context to a pathologised and denigrated one."

68 / p. 109: http://arxlv.org/abs/1002.0200 - Energy-Entanglement Relation for Quantum Energy Teleportation

69 / p. 111: The ESP Enigma written in 2009 by Dr. Dianne Hennacy Powell, a Harvard-trained medical doctor, is an excellent discussion of the need–based on the amount of available evidence–to take this kind of phenomena as seriously as any other

70 / p. 112: http://www.newscientist.com/article/mg15721254.900-beyond-reality–watching-information-at-play-in-the-quantuN-world-is-throwing-physicists-into-a-flat-spin-says-mark-buchanan.html

71 / p. 112: Please see chapter 24: Prove My Faith, p. 131.

72 / p. 114: Valerie Jamieson, New Scientist's features editor. – www.newscientist.com/article/mg21528840.600-reality-the-bedrock-of-it-all.html

73 / p. 114: www.newscientist.com/article/dn18669-first-quantuN-effects-seen-in-visible-object.html–www.livescience.com/38339-experiments-bolster-schrodingers-cat-idea.html

74 / p. 115: www.nytimes.com/2012/02/28/technology/ibN-inch-closer-on-quantuN-computer.html?_r=1&hpw

75 / p. 115: The speed of light, whose symbol is "c" = 299,792,458 meters per second, approximately 186,282 miles/s **76** / p. 115: www.kurzweilai.net/scorn-over-claiN-of-teleported-dna

77 / p. 115: www.hitachi.com/rd/research/em/abe.html. //en.wikipedia.org/wiki/Aharonov%E2%80%93Bohm_effect

78 / p. 116: Robert McLaughlin, A Different Universe. Written by a Nobel laureate physicist who sees classical Newtonian physics as emerging from a different and more fundamental set of physical laws.

79 / p. 116: "The many-world interpretation thus regards `the possible' as `the real', and asserts that we human beings are made to believe that `the possible' is not `the real', because we are locked inside one of the parallel universes." Diederik Aerts, Interpreting Quantum Particles as Conceptual Entities; Center Leo Apostel for Interdisciplinary Studies and Departments of Mathematics and Psychology, Vrije Universiteit

Brussel, 1160 Brussels, Belgium

80 / p. 116: "Prior to many-worlds, reality had been viewed as a single unfolding history. Many-worlds, rather, views reality as a many-branched tree, wherein every possible quantum outcome is realised." –http://en.wikipedia.org/wiki/Everett_many-worlds_interpretation

81 / p. 116: In his 2003 article published in the Scientific American magazine, Jacob Bekenstein summarized a current trend started by John Archibald Wheeler, which suggests that scientists may "regard the physical world as made of information, with energy and matter as incidentals." – http://en.wikipedia.org/wiki_Holographic_principle

82/ p. 116: http://www.world-science.net/othernews/111117_casimir

83 / p. 116: The Elegant Universe - PBS Nova.

84/ p. 119: Seth Speaks, by Jane Roberts

85/ p. 121: Please see chapter 36: Truth; page 195.

86 / p. 124: John Hanna, Sweeping anti-abortion bill goes to Kansas gov., Associated Press April 6, 2013

87 / p. 125: www.nytimes.com/2013/04/16/business/drugmakers-use-safety-rule-to-block-generics.html?pagewanted=2&hpw

88 / p. 131: University of Illinois at Urbana-Champaign (2013, June 26). ScienceDaily: www.sciencedaily.com/releases/2013/06//130626143106.htm

89 / p. 133: A person and I were on a train looking at a stark and rocky landscape streaming by. I commented that it was amazing to realize that these rocks were millions of years old. He replied that, according to his religion, they were only 4,000 years old. I then asked why did carbon dating place the rocks at a much, much, earlier time. He said that God arranged it so that they would look that old to the researchers.

90 / p. 133: Appendix, Write Makes Right - Writing Systems & Cultural Worldviews, C.C. Elian. 2011.

91 / p. 133: When God is Your Therapist. New York Times, April 13, 2013. T.M. Luhrmann.

92 / p. 134: "To hold, therefore, that there is no difference in matters of religion between forms that are unlike each other, and even contrary to each other, most clearly leads in the end to the rejection of all religion in both theory and practice. And this is the same thing as atheism, however it may differ from it in name." [Pope Leo XIII, Immortale Dei, 1885]

93 / p. 135: News.cnet.com/8301-17852_3-57580178-71/stephen-hawking-so-heres-how-it-all-happened-without-god/

94 / p. 137: Immordino-Yang, a professor of education, psychology and neuroscience at the University of Southern California. "What are we doing in schools to support kids turning inward?" – www.sciencedaily.com/releases/2012/07/120702184027.htm – Association for Psychological Science (2012, July 2). "Day dreaming good for you? Reflection is critical for development and well-being."

95 / p. 143: Please see chapter 27: The Mention of Dimensions; page 146.

96 / p. 145: List of 478 words with "form" in them: http://www.morewords.com/contains/form/

97 / p. 146: http://www.thefreedictionary.com/force

98 / p. 148: Barbara Stanwyck in *No Man of Her Own.*

99 / p. 150: British Psychological Society (BPS). "Face-to-face negotiations favor the powerful." ScienceDaily. ScienceDaily, 9 April 2013. <www.sciencedaily.com/releases/2013/04/130409211857.htm>.

100 / p. 153: Journal reference:, Physical Review Letters, doi.org/k3x
www.newscientist.com/article/dn23353-little-ripples-make-syrup-stringy.html

101 / p. 154: "This pleasure arises when certain signal substances, primarily dopamine, are released in the brain. But this reward system can be kidnapped by other rewarding substances, such as alcohol and abuser drugs like cocaine. They provide feelings of reward initially, but they are so strong that nerve cells in the system are rewired, and addiction occurs." – Uppsala University (2011, August 31). Faulty signaling in brain increases craving for sugar and drugs.
www.sciencedaily.com¬ /releases/2011/08/110830193855.htm

102 / p. 157: "Technique" has the root meaning of "skill" which it shares with the etymology of the word "art." – "... art (n.) early 13c., "skill as a result of learning or practice," from O.Fr. art (10c.), from L. artem (nom. ars) "work of art; practical skill; a business, craft," from PIE *ar-ti- (cf. Skt. rtih "manner, mode;...)" - http://www.etymonline.com/index.php?term=art - ©etymonline.com, Douglas Harper, 2010

103 / p. 163: opinionator.blogs.nytimes.com/2013/04/19/the-music-of-flow/ - The Music of 'Flow,' by Richard Carrick.

104 / p. 166: I like both cats and dogs.

105 / p. 166: "You are supposed to trust a doctor and you always think 'something like that would never happen to me', but that's not the case. It can happen to anyone and someone who is so sick to do something like that is very manipulative and it's not so cut and dry when it's happening." www.reddit.com/r/AMA/comments/1Difoh/amaa_i_was_sexually_assaulted_in_2005_by_my/

106 / p. 168: cityroom.blogs.nytimes.com/2013/04/21/pop-up-poets/On the Train, or at the Laundromat, Your Poem Begins ... Now. – New York Times, April 21, 2013, by Dusica Sue Malesevic

107 / p. 171: www.huffingtonpost.com/2014/06/23/divorce-reasons-n-5522650.html – "The Moment I Knew" slideshow.

108 / p. 172:
Prajapathi vai agre asset"
In the beginning was Prajapthi,
The Brahman-The God,
"Tasya Vag dvitiya Aseet"
With whom was the word;
"Vag vai parama Brahman"
And the word was verily the
Supreme Brahman - The God
-
John 1:1 states:
In the beginning was the word,
And the word was with God
And the word was God

109 / p. 172: "Noun" is another such word.

110/ p. 172: "grammar (n.) early 14c., gramarye (late 12c. in surnames), from Old French gramaire "learning," especially Latin and philology, "grammar, (magic) incantation, spells, mumbo-jumbo," "irregular semi-popular adoption" [OED] of Latin grammatica..."
– "Form grammar is from late 14c. Restriction to 'rules of language' is a post-classical development, but as this type of study was until 16c. limited to Latin, Middle English gramarye also

came to mean "learning in general, knowledge peculiar to the learned classes" (early 14c.), which included astrology and magic; hence the secondary meaning of "occult knowledge" (late 15c.), which evolved in Scottish into "glamor." www.etymonline.com/index.php?term=grammar. © 2001-2012 Douglas Harper.

111 / p. 173: From the movie Slander House, 1938

112 / p. 174: Sherlock Holmes: *The Woman in Green* with Basil Rathbone and Nigel Bruce; 1945.

113 / p. 175: https://www.newscientist.com/article/mg21829132-000-nana5-from-heaven-how-our-favourite-fruit-came-to-be/#

114 / p. 178: Francis Crick, The Astonishing Hypothesis, New York; Scribner, 1994. p. 3.

115 / p. 179: "The mean may often be confused with the median, mode or range. The mean is the arithmetic average of a set of values, or distribution; however, for skewed distributions, the mean is not necessarily the same as the middle value (median), or the most likely (mode). For example, mean income is skewed upwards by a small number of people with very large incomes, so that the majority have an income lower than the mean. By contrast, the median income is the level at which half the population is below and half is above..." http://en.wikipedia.org/wiki/Mean#Arithmetic_mean_.28AM.29

116 —DELETED

117 / p. 180: "Neuroscientists increasingly describe our behaviour as the result of a chain of cause-and-effect, in which one physical brain state or pattern of neural activity inexorably leads to the next, culminating in a particular action or decision. With little space for free choice in this chain of causation, the conscious, deliberating self seems to be a fiction." http://www.newscientist.com/article/mg21028081.200-grand-delusions-why-were-determined-to-be-free.html?

118 / p. 180: The researchers examined the brain recordings as the participants studied each word to home in on signals in the participant' brains that reflected the meanings of the words. About a second before the participants recalled each word, these same "meaning signals" that were identified during the study phase were spontaneously reactivated in the participants' brains."

University of Pennsylvania (2012, June 26). Mind reading from brain recordings? Neural fingerprints' of memory associations decoded. ScienceDaily. – http://www.sciencedaily.com¬/releases/2012/06/120626172721.htm

119/ p. 181: "One of the powerful things about this is that we don't have to endorse a stereotype to fall prey to its effects. The problem is that we are worried someone else believes it, which is not under our control. This idea of performing down to someone else's expectations can be really important." http://www.newscientist.com/article/mg21128200.200-psychologist-why-we-screw-up-when-the-heat-is-on.html?full=true&print=true

120 / p. 184: Frasier–Season 11, Episode one; 2003: "No Sex Please, We're Skittish."

121 / p. 185: Peter R. Harris, John M. Levine. Self-Affirmation Improves ProbleN-Solving under Stress. http://www.sciencedaily.com/releases 2013/05/130503132956.htmeter R. Harris, John M. Levine. Self-Affirmation Improves ProbleN-Solving under Stress. http://www.sciencedaily.com/releases 2013/05/130503132956.htm

122/ p. 186: "The finding 'makes very good sense,' said Dr. Neena Malik, a child psychologist at the University of Miami School of Medicine ... Young children may not understand the difference between what's real and not real, Malik said. When this happens, 'what you See: is going to feel real to you, and it's going to scare you,' she said."
"In addition, preschoolers don't have the skills to calm themselves down and soothe themselves after they become 'hyped up' emotionally by watching something intense. They may try to express their agitation physically, by crying or running around, Malik said."
http://www.livescience.com/14789-violent-tv-linked-kids-sleep-problems.html

123 / p. 186: Patients who practiced virtual activities improved more rapidly following a physical debilitation; players of sports or musical instruments who mentally practice improved almost as much as those who practiced in actual fact.

124/ p. 186: http://www.helium.com/items/529950-comparing-schizophrenia-and-multiple-personality-disorder

125 / p. 187: Joan Crawford; *Queen Bee*

126/ p. 195: *A Few Good Men*, 1992 movie. Directed by

Rob Reiner

127 / p. 196: www.bristol.ac.uk/biology/research/behaviour/vision/4D.html

128 / p. 199: The word "watch" is itself indicative of change as the more fundamental activity in space. It tells us to perceive (to watch) the differences around us such that we can agree to perceive the same given change in space.

129 / p. 199: The coordination of train schedules across different time zones in the late 1800s was the main reason for standardized time across the US.

130 / p. 200: http://www.scribd.com/doc/24699041/Perception-of-Time-in-Different-Cultures

131 / p. 200: Med.stanford.edu/ism/2013/april/numerals/html

132 / p. 209: en.wikipedia.org/wiki/Radical transparency

F

About the Author

C.C. Elian is a multi-media artist exploring how words and images shape our sense of self and of reality. She is the creator of various alternative writing systems, such as *Elian* script, the *Chromatic Alphabet*, and the *Elian SKU Alphabet* (ES-KUA); Elian is also the author of *Write Makes Right: Writing Systems & Cultural Worldviews*.

C.C. studied painting with Brice Marden at the School of Visual Arts, and worked with the NY designer Milton Glaser. She was graphic consultant for the Rolling Stones, Eric Clapton, and the Traveling Wilburys, as well as New York Times Magazine, New York Magazine, Movies, and others. She has exhibited from New York to Seattle, and her artworks can be found in various collections.

Elian has a *Bachelor of Social Sciences* from Washington State University, and was recipient of a WESTAF/NEA Fellowship for *Works on Paper*.

OS@ccelian.com
www.ccelian.com

ww.ingramcontent.com/pod-product-compliance
tning Source LLC
gne TN
010057110826
LV00028B/372